EXECUTIVE EDITOR
Natalie Earnheart

CREATIVE TEAM
Jenny Doan, Natalie Earnheart, Christine Ricks,
Tyler MacBeth, Mike Brunner, Lauren Dorton,
Jennifer Dowling, Dustin Weant, Jessica Toye,
Kimberly Forman, Denise Lane, Gunnar Forstrom

EDITORS & COPYWRITERS
Nichole Spravzoff, Camille Maddox,
Annie Gailbraith, David Litherland,
Julie Barber-Arutyunyan, Hillary Doan Sperry

SEWIST TEAM
Jenny Doan, Natalie Earnheart, Courtenay Hughes,
Carol Henderson, Denise Lane, Cassandra Ratliff,
Janice Richardson

PRINTING COORDINATOR
Rob Stoebener

PRINTING SERVICES
Walsworth Print Group
803 South Missouri
Marceline, MO 64658

LOCATIONS
Roger and Julie Hill, Hamilton, MO
Doug and Carol Henderson, Hamilton, MO
Jennifer Dowling, Hamilton, MO
Missouri Quilt Museum, Hamilton, MO

ADDITIONAL PHOTOGRAPHY
Lissa Claffey
Denise Kang
Karl MPhotography
Susan Hudson

SPECIAL THANKS TO
Craft in America
Mahota Textiles
The Navajo Quilt Project

CONTACT US
Missouri Star Quilt Company
114 N Davis
Hamilton, MO 64644
888-571-1122
info@missouriquiltco.com

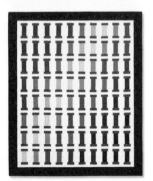

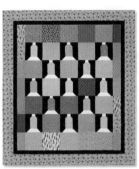

Oops! Sometimes we make mistakes. To find corrections to every issue of BLOCK go to: **msqc.co/corrections**

A note from Jenny

Dear Quilters,

Summer is here and I've been soaking up every moment in the sunshine. My hometown is lovely this time of year surrounded by spacious fields filled with ripening grain. The sun is shining brightly, we're smiling at each other—and we can actually see those smiles! The world seems to be a friendlier place and I am so thankful for all the progress we've made together. It's a cause for celebration! When I think back on summer last year, it hardly felt like a break even though I was at home the entire time. I'm sure you can relate. But we've made it through and look at where we're at now!

Progress can be hard to measure in small increments, but it's important every now and then to stop and look back at where you were and notice where you are now. And if you feel like you aren't where you want to be, always remember, that wherever you begin is okay. As C.S. Lewis said, "You can't go back and change the beginning, but you can start where you are and change the ending." That gives me great hope. I am grateful for experiences that help me to understand more, to love more, and to feel greater joy. Not all of those experiences are positive, but they can lead to growth if we allow them to teach us. Thank you for learning along with me and let's keep on making the world a more beautiful place.

Jenny

JENNY DOAN
MISSOURI STAR QUILT CO.

The Navajo Quilt Project

"Each time a man stands up for an ideal, or acts to improve the lot of others, or strikes out against injustice, he sends forth a tiny ripple of hope, and crossing each other from a million different centers of energy and daring, those ripples build a current that can sweep down the mightiest walls of oppression and resistance."
— *Robert F. Kennedy*

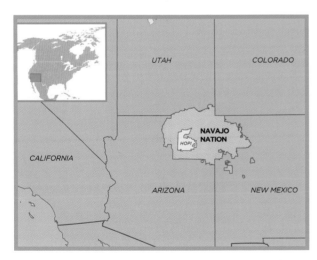

The Navajo Quilt Project began fifteen years ago after Kaari Meng Zabala, of French General, and her family moved from New York to Los Angeles. As they traveled across the picturesque high desert landscape, they passed through the Navajo Nation and stopped at trading posts along the way. They bought beautiful Navajo rugs at Hubbell, Toadlena, and Shonto.

Traveling through the Navajo Nation brought back memories of her childhood. Kaari said, "I have been visiting the Navajo Nation since I was a little girl and my mom and dad would take all seven of us out to Arizona and Utah to camp in Monument Valley. I had no idea that the seeds were being planted for a calling later in life."

"She told me that she had no access to fabric since there were no quilt or fabric shops on the reservation. I told her I would send her fabric from my collection—and that day, The Navajo Quilt Project began."

"I began meeting the locals and learning about a very simple way of life. I fell down the rabbit hole. I sat with weavers and spinners and natural dyers and learned more about history, craft, and landscape than I bargained for. I had no idea of the condition of life in the Navajo Nation."

Life on the reservation can be challenging. Many people live in poverty. Kaari said, "We have continued to visit this Native American territory, covering about 17,544,500 acres, and have found it to be a place of great beauty as well as great need. The population continues to disproportionately struggle with health problems, unemployment, and the effects of past uranium mining accidents." The Navajo Nation is located on portions of land in northeastern Arizona, southeastern Utah, and northwestern New Mexico. It is, in fact, larger than 10 U.S. states. This vast area was established in 1868 as a gathering place for the Diné and today it is home to about 250,000 residents. In Navajo, Diné means "the people."

MMIC Missing and Murdered Indigenous Children
made by Susan Hudson

Honoring Ledger Quilt made by Susan Hudson
POW: We are Prisoners of War in our own Country
MIA: For all the Missing and Murdered Relatives since 1492

African Star made by Susan Hudson

Kaari continues, "Five years ago, I met Fannie Mae Lincoln, a Navajo elder, at Griswold's Trading Post in Shiprock, New Mexico, while we were both buying wool. She asked me if I was a weaver and once we began our conversation, I learned that she was a weaver in the summer and a quilter in the winter. She told me that she had no access to fabric since there were no quilt or fabric shops on the reservation. I told her I would send her fabric from my collection—and that day, The Navajo Quilt Project began."

From that time, Kaari, along with many other quilters, have reached out to Navajo elders and helped to provide them with the essential quilting and sewing supplies they need for their livelihood. She said, "The Navajo Quilt Project gathers fabric and quilting supplies to donate to the quilters that live on the Navajo Nation. We also collect monetary donations and use it to purchase scissors, thread, and batting so that the elders can quilt in the winter and make beautiful, warm blankets for their families."

Susan Hudson, a revered Navajo quilter, explained the necessity of this project. "Some of us live hours away from a fabric store. Our reservation is so vast that the border towns can be over 100 miles away. The elders are on a fixed income and they can not afford to pay $11 a yard or buy an expensive sewing machine. A lot of the elders do not have running water, internet, indoor plumbing, or electricity. They sew by hand or use a treadle sewing machine.

Working with Kaari Zabala and The Navajo Quilt Project, the donations from people all over the country have made life a little easier for the elders."

When the elders receive donations, it is a cause for celebration. Susan said, "They get so excited when fabric is delivered safely and it's a chance for us to check up on them. It's like Christmas when they open up the bags and touch the fabric."

As The Navajo Quilt Project continues, there is an opportunity to help improve the lives of Navajo quilters. Kaari said, "I am hoping that this project will eventually provide an income to the grandmothers, mothers, and daughters who are able to make something that can then be used to sell or trade for supplies needed. Not all women who receive a box of fabric turn it into a quilt, many are sewing small stuffed animals and other items of comfort for children or students at the boarding schools."

So, how can we help support the work of Navajo quilters? It's easy. Donate your fabric and sewing supplies to The Navajo Quilt Project! Kaari said, "We work hard to get the word out about how to ship extra sewing supplies to the Navajo Nation so that the quilters can continue to sew. Our website, **frenchgeneral.com** has an updated list of addresses that are accepting donations."

"The Navajo Quilt Project gathers fabric and quilting supplies to donate to the quilters that live on the Navajo Nation. We also collect monetary donations and use it to purchase scissors, thread, and batting so that the elders can quilt in the winter and make beautiful, warm blankets for their families."

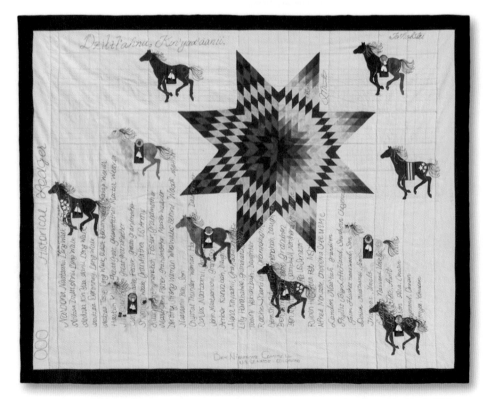

*Star Among the Shunka Wakann
made by Susan Hudson*

Donate to
The Navajo Quilt Project at:
**frenchgeneral.com/products/
navajoquiltproject**

Get The Navajo Quilt Project tote:
**frenchgeneral.com/products/
the-navajo-quilt-project**

"We always ask people to send their donations to USPS and to include a self-addressed/stamped envelope so that they will receive a confirmation note once items are received. We also sell Navajo Quilt Project tote bags which help with shipping supplies as well as purchasing supplies in need on our website."

As you start to sort through your stash, you might be wondering, what kind of donations do Navajo quilters need? The Navajo Quilt Project collects and distributes fabric, scraps, finished quilts, unfinished quilt tops, blankets, batting, and sewing supplies including scissors, rotary cutters, cutting mats, books, yarn, and notions. Kaari said, "Because there is so much poverty in the Navajo Nation, almost anything is appreciated and used. I never say no to any donation!" If you have any questions, you can contact Kaari at **notions@frenchgeneral.com**. This project only works because quilters like you care about our sisters in the Navajo Nation.

Donations to The Navajo Quilt Project

Quilts Designed from Dreams
Susan Hudson

Susan Hudson
photography by Lissa Claffey | courtesy of Craft in America

Ya a' tey, *(Hello)*
Susan Hudson yii niish yii *(I am Susan Hudson)*
Kee yah aa' niih nish lii' *(I am from the Towering House Clan)*
Deshchii' Nii ii' ee baa' shish chiin' *(and the Apache People Clan)*
Taabaa ii' ee' daa' shi chei *(My maternal grandfather is from the Water's Edge Clan)*
Naaki' Din na ii' ee daa' shi Naah lii' *(My paternal grandfather is from the Mexican People Clan)*
I live in Tooh Haltsooi *(Sheep Springs, New Mexico)* **on the Navajo Reservation.**
Hello to all my relations and friends around the world!

Meet Susan Hudson, a Navajo quilter from Sheep Springs, New Mexico, Navajo Reservation. She is proud to be of the Diné (Navajo) people. Her work as a quilter, and an activist, is to tell the stories of her people. These stories are woven into the fabric of her being so seamlessly that she dreams about them often and her beautiful quilt designs come from her dreams. This is the motivation that goes into everything she creates. Her quilts will continue on, telling her stories and telling her ancestors' stories, long after she has finished creating them. As she has said, "What did you do today to honor your ancestors?"

29 Warriors made by Susan Hudson
photography Denise Kang | courtesy of Craft in America

Susan began sewing when she was around nine years old. At first she remarked that it may seem unusual to some to see a person of her tribal affiliation quilting, as many are weavers and make beautiful rugs and baskets. She said, "My mother taught me how to sew out of necessity, since we were so poor she couldn't afford to buy us clothes. She learned how to sew while she was at Toadlena Boarding School. The scraps of fabric that were left over from the clothes that she would resize for us, we would make into scrap quilts." At first Susan struggled to enjoy sewing as her mistakes were corrected sternly by her mother, but after learning more about her mother's history and the cruelties she experienced while at the boarding school, she understood why. In time, she learned to embrace quilting and make it her own. Susan said, "I'm only one generation removed from my mother's traumatic experience of those schools, so I sew in honor of her, my grandmother, and my ancestors."

Quilting hasn't always been a part of Navajo culture, but it became a part of their tradition after the Navajo people, and many other Native American tribes, were taught how to sew by European missionaries and, later on, in boarding schools, beginning as early as 1860. Susan continued, "The forced removal of indigenous children from their families and being sent to boarding schools [was] where they were forced to sew. My mother said that she wonders what she would have become if she didn't go to a boarding school. She was taught to be a servant." Sadly, this story is not unique.

In Indian Residential Schools, children were made to cut their hair, wear American-style uniforms, change their given names to English-language names, and they were forbidden to speak their native languages. They were often treated poorly, forced to do manual labor, and many were abused and even killed. Families who refused to send their children to these schools were punished, some fathers even spending time in jail. It was only in 1978 that the Indian Child Welfare Act was passed, which allowed families to legally refuse to place their children in boarding schools.

Susan Hudson at her sewing machine
photography by Lissa Claffey | courtesy of Craft in America

Star Horse Vest made by Susan Hudson

It is knowing this history that helps to set the stage for Susan's quilts. They come from a deep tradition of survival, perseverance, and hope for the future. With her inspiring quilt designs she has been able to overcome and to be an advocate for others, inspiring them to stand up and tell their stories, too.

She said, "In order to be able to tell many stories with my quilts they have to be able to evoke emotions in people and to speak for themselves. From the very first dream that I have been blessed with, to sew it into reality, to the very last stitch, I am able to convey the emotional impact that the quilt had on me."

"To ensure that our ancestors' stories are never forgotten, I have made a mark on the Native quilting world, and opened the doors for those that will come after me. To show that it has taken generations of Native quilters to help me become the artist that I am. By taking quilting to another level, I have combined quilting and ledger art, consequently becoming a 'Contemporary Ledger Artist.'"

"By using the best quality materials, my quilts are able to withstand the elements and time and to ensure that our descendants will be able to look at my quilts. The honoring of our ancestors—those that lived, cried, shed blood, and died—so we are able to be here and to tell their stories."

Creating a quilt for Block was an unusual task for Susan, as we have learned that her quilts don't come to her from outside sources. That is why we are especially honored to be able to feature her work here and learn more about her story. We are able to gain even more insight about her as she explains her quilting process.

As she begins a quilt, she said, "Due to the process which I go through, my quilts are integrated with ledger art, my quilts tell a story, so I really don't use a pattern that you can find in books, stores, or the internet. I get them from dreams."

To make a quilt, it isn't as simple as picking out a pattern and buying the fabric for Susan. She explains, "It is around an 18-month process from the beginning of the dreams, to choosing of the fabric, to trying to make my templates."

Susan chooses her color palette carefully. She paints with fabric and considers carefully the look that she is trying to create. She said, "The colors of the fabric that I use depend on my quilt. If I am doing something around my 4-times or 3-times great-grandmother's time, I will use Civil War, Stonehenge, Kona Cotton, and material that looks like wood. Their time is during the 'Long Walk of the Navajos' and 'The Boarding School Era.'"

She said, "For my missing and murdered indigenous people, I will use red and yellow. As for my star quilts, it depends on the colors I am using. I like to use colors that will pop when I use black or brown as the background."

When she begins sewing her quilts, she has a few tips and tricks. "Since my ledger quilts have a lot of machine appliqué, my best tip is to have a few pairs of tweezers. I like to pick them up from discount stores, they have them in slant edge and narrow edges. I find them better than the ones they sell at fabric stores." These small tweezers help her work more skillfully with her intricate designs as she designs and sews. But Susan is not stuck on perfection as she quilts. She has said, "In the traditional Navajo way, the only one who is perfect is the Great Spirit and the Spirit helpers, and so I do make a lot of mistakes."

Most of her quilts use machine appliqué and she explains her technique, "I use a lot of machine appliqué, for me I use Heat n Bond Lite, lots of different shades of gray in my bobbin, my favorite iron, tweezers, small sharp scissors, and sometimes I use a glue stick. What I do is, after I have ironed the fabric onto the Heat n Bond Lite, I will cut out all the pieces. Then I start layering the fabric, gently ironing the pieces, but not fully bonding them together, just

Susan Hudson with her quilt, 29 Warriors
photography by Lissa Claffey | courtesy of Craft in America

enough to tack them down. Then begins the fun part. I start to lay all the fabric down and move pieces if needs be."

As she creates her pictorial ledger quilts, she does occasionally encounter quilter's block, as we all do. But this is how she deals with challenges. She said, "Some quilters don't like to use the word 'stuck,' but I do get stuck and my mind doesn't know what to do next. I put the quilt in the other room and just walk away. Usually later that evening I will dream about it and will know how to fix it or just do it another way. I believe that the quilt tells me where to place the pieces of fabric; if it is not supposed to be placed there, I will become stuck." She allows the quilt to guide her as she creates her masterpiece and the end result speaks for itself. It is exactly what it needs to be.

When Susan is done creating her quilts, they are often displayed in museums. In fact, Susan just won Best of Division in Weaving and Textiles, 1st Place in Weaving and Textiles, and The Idyllwild Arts Imagination Award at the Heard Museum Indian Show for her quilt "MMIW (Missing and Murdered Indigenous Women), The Tree Of Many Dresses." This quilt seeks to tell the story of the epidemic of missing and murdered Indigenous women and girls.

She said, "My agreement with every museum is that if my children, my grandchildren, my descendants want to see a quilt, that they open the door to let them in because this is

The Indigenous Children Want to Know Why, made by Susan Hudson
photography by Denise Kang | courtesy of Craft in America

their legacy too." Two of her grandchildren are also her business partners. She says, "My grandchildren have seen the process that goes into making my quilts. A lot of times they have seen pieces of the quilt on the floor as I am laying it out and hanging off the table when I am machine quilting. So when they see people at the museum wearing white gloves handling the quilt, they are amazed at how careful people are with my quilts. Especially when my quilts are displayed in museums, the different lighting and the enclosure that surrounds the quilt, so people won't touch them."

Giving gifts is a part of Navajo culture, and Susan enjoys this part of quilting. She said, "People always ask me, 'Don't you feel bad when you give them away?'" And she replied, "No, that's what they're for. They're stories. I made them for a reason. They're going to go someplace and go to the right place and they're going to be shown and the story's going to go on."

The quilt that Susan made for Block Magazine was about her connection to Kaari Zabala of French General. Susan said, "I chose this pattern to represent the admiration that I have for Kaari, her tenacity, her caring for our elders, and most of all, her beautiful heart. I am so honored that she allowed me to use her new line La Vie Boheme. The backing has a special meaning to me, when I look at it it reminds me of a Navajo Turquoise Pin, like the ones that the elders wear when they dress up to go to town. The star is to represent the Morning Star, the first star of the day, the beginning of a new day."

E'toile de France Quilt

designed by Susan Hudson

materials

QUILT SIZE
92" x 92"

BLOCK SIZE
58½" unfinished, 58" finished

QUILT TOP
6 different fabrics are needed for the star & pieced borders
- Fabric A - ½ yard
- Fabric B - ¾ yard
- Fabric C - 1 yard
- Fabric D - 1 yard
- Fabric E - 1¼ yards
- Fabric F - 1 yard

4½ yards background fabric
   - includes borders

BINDING
¾ yard

BACKING
8½ yards - vertical seam(s)
or 2¾ yards of 108" wide

SAMPLE QUILT
La Vie Boheme by French General for Moda Fabrics

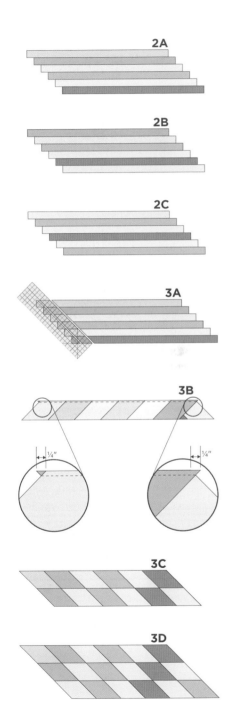

2A

2B

2C

3A

3B

3C

3D

1 assign & cut

Assign a letter to your fabrics A-F. You may find it helpful to create a little chart with fabric swatches for yourself to keep track.

Tip: Starch your fabrics before cutting to prevent any skewing.

From fabric A, cut (2) 2½" strips across the width of the fabric.

From fabric B, cut (4) 2½" strips across the width of the fabric.

From fabric C, cut (6) 2½" strips across the width of the fabric.

From fabric D, cut (8) 2½" strips across the width of the fabric.

From fabric E, cut (10) 2½" strips across the width of the fabric.

From fabric F, cut (6) 2½" strips across the width of the fabric.

Set the remainder of fabrics A-F aside for the pieced border.

From the background fabric:
• Cut (1) 25" strip across the width of the fabric. Subcut (1) 25" square. Subcut the square twice on the diagonal to yield a **total of 4** triangles.

• Cut (2) 17¾" strips across the width of the fabric. Subcut a **total of (4)** 17¾" strips.

• Set the remaining fabric aside for the borders.

2 sew strip sets

Select 1 fabric A, 1 fabric B, 1 fabric C, 1 fabric D, 1 fabric E, and 1 fabric F strip and arrange them in that order. Offset the ends of the strips by 2½" and sew them together lengthwise. Press. We'll refer to this as strip set 1. **Make 2**. **2A**

Select 1 fabric B, 1 fabric C, 1 fabric D, 1 fabric E, 1 fabric F, and 1 fabric E strip and arrange them in that order. Offset the ends of the strips by 2½" and sew them together lengthwise. Press. We'll refer to this as strip set 2. **Make 2**. **2B**

Select 1 fabric C, 1 fabric D, 1 fabric E, 1 fabric F, 1 fabric E, and 1 fabric D strip and arrange them in that order. Offset the ends of the strips by 2½" and sew them together lengthwise. Press. We'll refer to this as strip set 3. **Make 2**. **2C**

3 make star legs

Use a ruler with a 45° angle mark. Align the 45° mark on your ruler with a seam line of the strip set. Cut a **total of (16)** 2½" units from each kind of strip set—1, 2, and 3. Keep these units together with the like strip set units. **3A**

Place a strip set 1 unit atop a strip set 2 unit and offset the ends by ¼". Sew the 2 units together and press. **3B 3C**

In the same manner, sew a strip set 3 unit to the bottom and press. **Make 16**. **3D**

Pick up 2 of the units you just made and rotate the bottom unit 180° as shown. Similar to before, offset the units by ¼" and sew them together. Press. **Make 8** star legs. **3E 3F**

4 sew the quilt center

Note: Because we are making Y-seams, backstitching is important to secure the ends of the seams where other seams aren't crossing over. Backstitch at the end of each seam about ¼" before reaching the edge of the fabric.

Pair 2 star legs, right sides facing, with like-fabrics touching. Sew them together starting at the center point and stopping ¼" before reaching the outer corner (as indicated by the red dot on the diagram), backstitch. Press. **4A**

Sew (1) 17¾" background square to 1 side of a star leg, starting and stopping ¼" from each end. Don't forget to backstitch. Repeat to sew the adjacent side of the square to the adjacent star leg. **Make 4** corner units. **4B**

Sew 2 corner units together, starting at the center point and ending ¼" before reaching the outer edge of the star leg, backstitch. Press. **Make 2**. **4C**

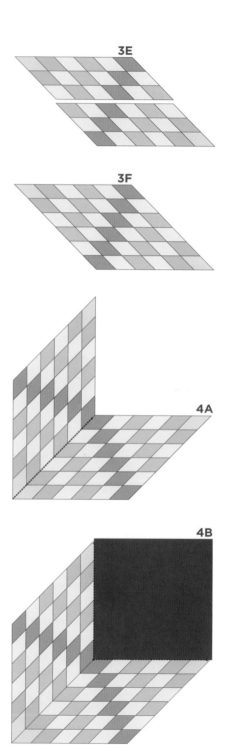

4C

4D

Nest the center seam and sew the 2 units together to complete the star. Start and stop ¼" from each end of the star legs, backstitch. Press. **4D**

Sew 1 of the short sides of a background triangle to 1 of the remaining edges of a star leg, starting ¼" from the innermost part of the star leg and backstitching. Press. Repeat on the other short side of the triangle to attach the background triangle to the star. Repeat to add the 3 remaining background triangles to the star. **4E**

Measure 29¼" from the center seams in each direction and square the quilt center to 58½".

Block Size: 58½" unfinished, 58" finished

5 inner border

From the background fabric, cut (15) 4½" strips across the width of the fabric and set the remainder of the fabric aside for the pieced border. Sew them together to form 1 long strip. Cut the inner borders from this strip and then set the remainder of the long strip aside for the outer border. Refer to Borders (pg. 118) in the Construction Basics to measure, cut, and attach the borders. The strip lengths are approximately 58½" for the sides and 66½" for the top and bottom.

6 pieced border

Note: Refer to Borders (pg. 118) in the Construction Basics to measure, cut, and attach the borders. If your quilt measures differently than 66½" x 66½" with the inner borders attached, you can adjust the sizes of the background rectangles you cut below to account for any variation.

From each of fabrics A-F, cut (2) 5" strips across the width of the fabric. Arrange 1 strip of each fabric in alphabetical order. Sew the strips together lengthwise and then press. **Make 2** strip sets. Cut the strip sets into a **total of (16)** 5" segments. **6A**

Select 2 strip set segments and rotate 1 segment 180° and then sew them together. Press. **Make 8**. **6B**

Sew 2 of the units together end-to-end and press. **Make 4**. **6C**

From the background fabric, cut (3) 9½" strips across the width of the fabric.
- From 2 of the strips, subcut (1) 9½" x 21½" and (1) 9½" square from each strip.

- From 1 of the strips, subcut (2) 9½" x 12½" rectangles.

Sew a 9½" x 12½" background rectangle to the left end of a pieced unit. Press. **Make 2** side border strips that measure approximately 66½" long. **6D**

22

Sew a 9½" square to 1 end of a remaining pieced unit and a 9½" x 21½" background rectangle to the other. Press. **Make 2** borders for the top and bottom of the quilt that measure approximately 84½" long. **6E**

Refer to Borders (pg. 118) in the Construction Basics and sew the pieced borders to the quilt top.

7 outer border

Pick up the remainder of the long strip that you set aside earlier and cut the outer borders from this strip. Refer to Borders (pg. 118) in the Construction Basics to measure, cut, and attach the borders. The strip lengths are approximately 84½" for the sides and 92½" for the top and bottom.

8 quilt & bind

Layer the quilt with batting and backing, then quilt. See Construction Basics (pg. 118) to finish your quilt.

The Italian Cotton Makers
Happy Little Spools Quilt

Some folks adore Italy for its architecture, fine wine, and high fashion. Others swoon over made-from-scratch ravioli and classic Italian opera. But for quilters, Italy is the home of something much more special: Aurifil, the maker of the best thread on earth.

Aurifil's founder, Angelo Gregotti, started his career in embroidery. His company, Studio Auriga, began producing designs for an industrial embroidery machine in 1957. Angelo was always on the hunt for innovation, and he traveled the world seeking fresh ideas and new technology. Somewhere along the way, Angelo became interested in thread. Really, really good thread.

In 1983, Angelo joined forces with a former school mate, Adolfo Veronelli, to embark on a journey to produce the finest thread on the market. This new thread had to be top-quality, made from the very best cotton; it had to be strong and durable with a rich, beautiful sheen. And that's exactly what they created.

Aurifil thread is manufactured in Milan, but its journey begins almost 2,000 miles away in the Mako region of Egypt. The climate and soil of the Nile delta provide ideal conditions for cotton with an extra long fiber staple, a must-have for thread that is smooth and strong. These super-soft cotton bolls are handpicked and shipped to Italy where they undergo a fifteen-step transformation from fluff to thread. Here are just a few highlights:

Aurifl thread is mercerized, or treated with caustic soda to shrink the fibers for greater strength and luster. It is dyed 270 different glorious colors from the softest white to the deepest magenta and dipped in a paraffin oil to prepare the thread to glide through your machine like a swan through water.

The end result is a spool of thread that is strong, vibrant, and made to last. It doesn't break, it doesn't tangle, and it doesn't shed lint inside your sewing machine. Best of all, a quilt made with Aurifil thread is sure to weather picnics, wash cycles, and endless cuddles for years and years to come.

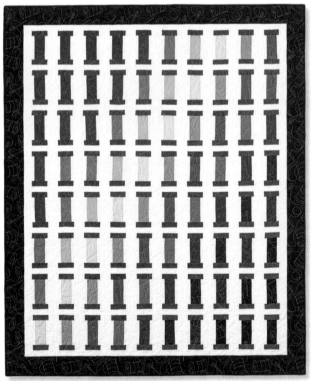

materials

QUILT SIZE
58" x 68"

BLOCK SIZE
4½" x 7" unfinished,
4" x 6½" finished

QUILT TOP
1 package of 5" solid squares
¾ yard accent fabric
2½ yards background fabric*
 - includes sashing and
   inner border

BORDER
¾ yard

BINDING
¾ yard

BACKING
3¾ yards - horizontal seam(s)

__Note:__ 1 roll of 1½" background strips and ¾ yard background fabric can be substituted. You will need to cut (6) additional 1½" background strips and add them to your roll, then follow directions for the remaining (12) 1" strips.

SAMPLE QUILT
Kona Cotton - Bright Rainbow Palette by Robert Kaufman

2A

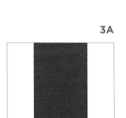

3A

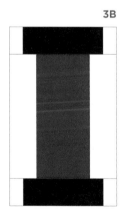

3B

1 cut

Set (2) 5" print squares aside for another project. Cut each remaining 5" print square in half to create a **total of (80)** 2½" x 5" rectangles.

From the accent fabric, cut (6) 3½" strips across the width of the fabric.

From the background fabric, cut:
- (46) 1½" strips across the width of the fabric. Subcut 20 strips into 1½" x 5" rectangles for a **total of 160**. Set the remaining strips aside for the sashing and inner border.

- (12) 1" strips across the width of the fabric. Set aside for the strip sets.

2 make strip sets

Sew a 1" background strip to both long sides of an accent strip. Press. **Make 6**. Cut each strip set into (28) 1½" increments for a **total of 160** spool ends. **2A**

3 block construction

Sew a 1½" x 5" background rectangle to either side of a 2½" x 5" print rectangle. Press. **3A**

Sew a spool end to the top and bottom of the print unit as shown. Press. **Make 80** blocks. **3B**

Block Size: 4½" x 7" unfinished, 4" x 6½" finished

4 make sashing

From the 1½" background strips set aside previously, cut 12 strips into (6) 1½" x 7" vertical sashing rectangles for a **total of 72**. Sew the remaining 14 strips together to create 1 long strip. Set aside for the horizontal sashing and inner border.

5 arrange & sew

Refer to the diagram on page 29 as needed to lay out your blocks in **8 rows of 10**. Sew the blocks together in rows with a vertical sashing rectangle between each block. Press.

1 Sew a 1" background strip to both long sides of an accent strip. Press. Make 6. Cut each strip set into (28) 1½" increments for a total of 160 spool ends.

2 Sew a 1½" x 5" background rectangle to either side of a 2½" x 5" print rectangle. Press.

3 Sew a spool end to the top and bottom of the print unit as shown. Press. Make 80 blocks.

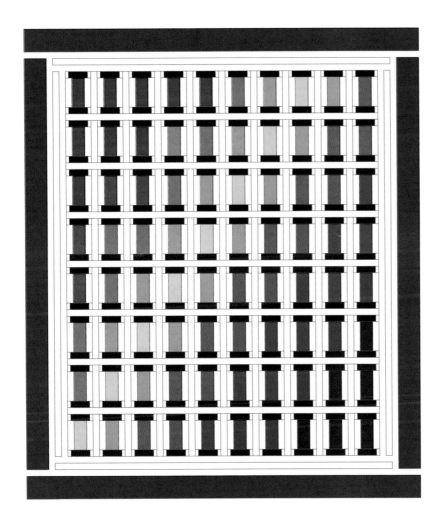

6 inner border

Trim the inner borders from the long background strip sewn earlier. Refer to Borders (pg. 118) in the Construction Basics to measure, cut, and attach the inner borders. The strip lengths are approximately 59½" for the sides and 51½" for the top and bottom.

7 outer border

Cut (6) 4" strips across the width of the border fabric. Sew the strips together to make 1 long strip. Trim the borders from this strip. Refer to Borders (pg. 118) in the Construction Basics to measure, cut, and attach the outer borders. The strip lengths are approximately 61½" for the sides and 58½" for the top and bottom.

8 quilt & bind

Layer the quilt with batting and backing, then quilt. See Construction Basics (pg. 118) to finish your quilt.

Once Upon a Time
Lady of the Lake Quilt

Great stories are like heirloom quilts; they are passed from generation to generation, growing more cozy and beloved as time goes by. So, come sit by the fire, my friends. Wrap a quilt 'round your shoulders, and listen to the legend of King Arthur and the Lady of the Lake.

We begin in 5th century England, with King Uther Pendragon and his infant son, Arthur. These are dark and perilous days, and the threat of enemy invasion is constant. Fearing for Arthur's safety, the king entrusts little Arthur to Merlin the wizard, who hides the young prince in a faraway village where no one will guess his identity.

Far from the privilege of his royal home, poor Arthur grows into a scrawny and awkward young man. He is bullied, unloved, and unimportant. Then, one day, King Pendragon is poisoned by enemies and dies without an heir to the throne. A rumor spreads of an enchanted sword embedded in a stone at Westminster: If any man can remove the sword, he will be declared king.

For years, men strong and bold take turns pulling at that sword, but they all fail. The sword is stuck tight. Until one day, quite by accident, an unsuspecting Arthur picks up the sword with ease. It slides right out in his feeble hands, and he is declared King of all Britain. But that is not the end of the story, for now we meet the Lady of the Lake, and things get really exciting.

The Lady of the Lake is an enchantress who lives in an underwater castle. Her lake surrounds the mystical island of Avalon. When a band of local kings attempt a rebellion against King Arthur, the Lady of the Lake emerges from her magical lake to arm him with a powerful sword named Excalibur.

With Excalibur in his hands, Arthur cannot be defeated and, with its scabbard on his belt, he is protected from all wounds. Arthur carries Excalibur into battle, defeats his enemies, and begins his storied reign with Queen Guinevere and the Knights of the Round Table at his side.

I'd love to say "they lived happily ever after," but that's not quite true. After years of adventure and victory, the magical scabbard is stolen and Arthur is mortally wounded by his own nephew, Mordred.

As Arthur lay dying, the sword Excalibur fell from his hands. His loyal knight, Sir Bedivere, was under orders to take the sword and cast it into the lake should the king ever fall. After first hesitating and thinking to keep the sword for the next king, eventually Sir Bedivere relented and gave it to the water. Breaking the surface, the hand of the Lady of the Lake arose, caught the sword as he threw it, and took it back to the watery depths.

materials

QUILT SIZE
70" x 70"

BLOCK SIZE
10½" unfinished, 10" finished

QUILT TOP
1 package of 10" print squares
1 package of 10" background
squares

BORDER
1¼ yards

BINDING
¾ yard

BACKING
4½ yards - vertical seam(s)
or 2¼ yards of 108" wide

OTHER
Clearly Perfect Slotted
Trimmers A and B or
Bloc Loc 6½" Square Up Ruler

SAMPLE QUILT
Gratitude and Grace by Kim
Diehl for Henry Glass

BONUS *Find a wider range of project sizes in your digital issue!*

1A

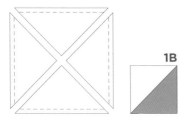

1B

2A

2B

1 make large half-square triangles

Set (6) 10" print squares and (6) 10" background squares aside for another project.

Layer a background square atop a print square, right sides together. Sew around the perimeter. **Make 36**. **1A**

Set 27 sewn squares in a variety of prints aside for section 2.

Cut each of the 9 remaining squares twice diagonally. Use trimmer A to square each unit to 5½" then press open—or press, then square to 5½" if not using the trimmer. Each set of sewn squares will yield 4 large half-square triangles for a **total of 36**. **1B**

2 make small half-square triangles

Measure and mark both vertical and horizontal center lines on each of the 27 sewn squares. Sew on either side of the lines just marked. **2A 2B**

Cut each of the squares along the marked lines, then cut each smaller square twice diagonally. Use trimmer B to square each unit to 3" then press open—or press, then square to 3" if not using the trimmer. Each set of sewn squares will yield 16 small half-square triangles for a **total of 432**. **2C**

3 block construction

Tip: Use different prints throughout the block construction for a scrappy look.

Sew 2 small half-square triangles together as shown. Press. **Make 72** short units. **3A**

Sew 4 small half-square triangles as shown. Press towards the left. **Make 72** long units. **3B**

Sew a short unit to either side of a large half-square triangle as shown. Press towards the right. **3C**

Sew a long unit to the top and bottom of the unit just made. Press. Repeat to **make 36** blocks. **3D**

Block Size: 10½" unfinished, 10" finished

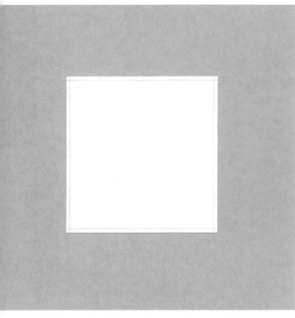

1 Layer a background square atop a print square, right sides together. Sew around the perimeter. Make 36.

2 Cut each of the 9 remaining squares twice diagonally. Square each unit to 5½".

3 Measure and mark both vertical and horizontal center lines on each of 27 sewn squares. Sew on either side of the lines just marked

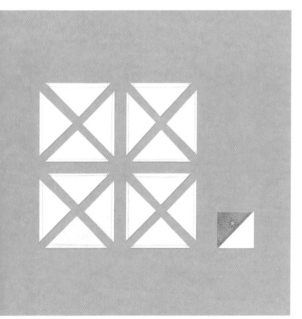

4 Cut each of the squares along the marked lines, then cut each smaller square twice diagonally. Square each unit to 3".

5 Sew 2 small half-square triangles together as shown. Press. Make 72 short units. Sew 4 small half-square triangles as shown. Press towards the left. Make 72 long units.

6 Sew a short unit to either side of a large half-square triangle as shown. Press towards the right. Sew a long unit to the top and bottom of the unit. Press. Make 36.

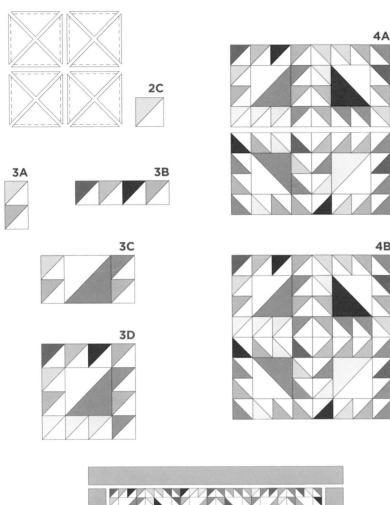

2C

3A

3B

3C

3D

4A

4B

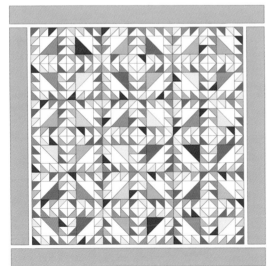

4 make the diamond units

Arrange 4 blocks in a 4-patch formation as shown. Notice that the background corners create a center diamond. Sew the blocks together in 2 rows. Press in opposite directions. Nest the seams and sew the blocks together. Press. **Make 9.** **4A 4B**

5 arrange & sew

Refer to the diagram below as needed to lay out your diamond units in **3 rows of 3**. Sew the units together in rows. Press the rows in opposite directions. Nest the seams and sew the rows together. Press.

6 border

Cut (7) 5½" strips across the width of the border fabric. Sew the strips together to make 1 long strip. Trim the borders from this strip. Refer to Borders (pg. 118) in the Construction Basics to measure, cut, and attach the borders. The strip lengths are approximately 60½" for the sides and 70½" for the top and bottom.

7 quilt & bind

Layer the quilt with batting and backing, then quilt. After the quilting is complete, see Construction Basics (pg. 118) to finish your quilt.

Memories from Quilt Town, USA
Mother's Choice Remake Quilt

Every year, quilters across the globe make the trek to Hamilton, Missouri to shop, sew, and create sweet memories at the home of Missouri Star. What is it like to visit Quilt Town, U.S.A? We asked quilters to share their favorite Hamilton moments:

"I visited one week ago. It was fabulous! The amount of fabric was overwhelming, the quilts on display were magnificent, and everyone on staff was pleasant and very helpful. The streets were lined with beautiful baskets of flowers and the whole atmosphere was relaxed and wonderful. It's a must visit for all quilters!" — *Dotty Damm Ernst*

"My husband and I just returned from our first trip to Hamilton. It was glorious! I came prepared with a two-page shopping list; we left town with a low-riding SUV. My husband helped pick out batiks for my next project and find the missing issues of BLOCK Magazine to complete my collection. After that, I left him in Man's Land to rest in a leather recliner, watch tv on a big screen, and sip a cup of 'really good' coffee. After a couple of days of intense shopping, we were ready to take our treasures home. We stepped out of the last shop all set to hit the road when my husband called out "Hold up! Isn't that your BFF?" I turned to look down the sidewalk … and there was Jenny with Chuck the Duck! Jenny greeted me with a big hug. Then, noticing my husband's Marines shirt, she thanked him for his service. She shared a story about the Quilting Marine, a 20-year veteran who quilts to ease symptoms of PTSD. Jenny is just as sweet and wonderful in person as she seems in her tutorials. Meeting her was the highlight of my trip!" — *Kim Schoffstall*

"I went to a retreat by myself this year. My brother and his wife were worried I wouldn't have fun all alone. I told them not to worry, I would be with quilters, and quilters are the friendliest people you will ever meet! I had so much fun with the ladies at the sewing tables next to mine. It was like a family reunion for a week. They told me if I quilted as much as I shopped, my quilt would be finished. They were right. Some people call Hamilton 'the Disney World of quilting,' but it's not. It's BETTER! I am looking forward to another retreat next year. I would have gone this summer, but … I'm going to Disney with the family instead. I will be wishing I was back in Hamilton the whole time!" — *Alice Willis*

"We were on our way to the Truman Presidential Library in Independence, Missouri, when my husband said, 'Hmmm. MSQC can't be too far.' And off we went! Somehow our GPS took us the back way, and we couldn't find the shops. We were in a blinding rainstorm, and my husband pulled into what looked like a small office building. Soaking wet, I ran inside to ask directions. A very nice lady obliged, then said, 'Would you like to meet Jenny?' Somehow, I had stumbled upon one of Jenny's studios. Although she was busy talking with someone else, Jenny came over to greet me and insisted on a photo. What a wonderful memory of my time in Hamilton! We are planning another trip this summer." — *Joyce Lalacona Ross*

materials

QUILT SIZE
63" x 75"

BLOCK SIZE
12½" unfinished, 12" finished

QUILT TOP
1 roll of 2½" print strips
1 roll of 2½" background strips

INNER BORDER
½ yard

OUTER BORDER
1¾ yards - includes block
    center squares

BINDING
¾ yard

BACKING
4¾ yards - vertical seam(s)
    or 2½ yards of 108" wide

SAMPLE QUILT
Cora by Tessie Fay for
Windham Fabrics

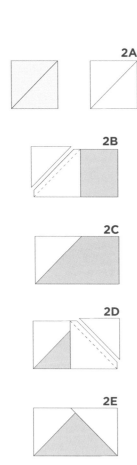

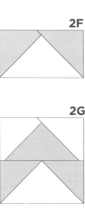

2A

2B

2C

2D

2E

2F

2G

1 cut

From the outer border fabric, cut (3) 4½" strips across the width of the fabric. Subcut a **total of (20)** 4½" squares from the strips. Set the remainder of the fabric aside for the outer border.

From (15) 2½" background strips, cut a **total of (240)** 2½" squares and set them aside for section 3. Set the remaining background strips aside for section 2.

2 make the chevron units

Select a 2½" print strip and a 2½" background strip. From each strip cut (4) 2½" x 4½" rectangles and (8) 2½" squares.

Mark a diagonal line once corner to corner on the reverse side of each square. **2A**

Place a marked background square on the left end of a print rectangle. Sew on the marked line and then trim the excess fabric ¼" away from the sewn seam. Press. **2B 2C**

Place another marked background square on the right end of the same print rectangle. Sew, trim, and press as before. **Make 4** print flying geese. **2D 2E**

In a similar fashion, **make 4** background flying geese using the marked print squares and background rectangles. **2F**

Sew a print flying geese unit to the top of a background flying geese unit. Press. **Make 4** to complete a set. **2G**

Repeat to **make 20** sets of chevron units. Keep the sets organized together.

3 make the corner units

Select a 2½" print strip and cut (4) 2½" x 4½" rectangles and (4) 2½" squares from the strip.

Mark a diagonal line once corner to corner on the reverse side of 160 background squares. **3A**

Sew an unmarked 2½" background square to a 2½" print square. Press. **3B**

Sew a 2½" x 4½" print rectangle to the bottom of the unit. Press. **3C**

Lay 2 marked background squares on the opposite print corners of the unit and sew on the marked lines. Trim the excess fabric ¼" away from the sewn seams. Press. **Make 4** to complete a set. **3D 3E**

Repeat to **make 20** sets of corner units. Keep the sets organized together.

4 block construction

Select 1 set of chevron units and 1 set of corner units. The 2 sets you select should feature different prints. Pick up a 4½" border fabric square and arrange the units in 3 rows of 3. Sew the units together in rows. Press. **4A**

Nest the seams and sew the rows together. Press. **Make 20**. **4B**

Block Size: 12½" unfinished, 12" finished

Mother's Choice
Remake Quilt

1 Mark a diagonal line on the reverse side of a square and lay it atop a rectangle as shown. Sew on the marked line and trim the excess fabric. Press.

2 Repeat on the opposite side of the rectangle to create a flying geese unit. Make 4. Repeat using marked print squares on the ends of 4 background rectangles.

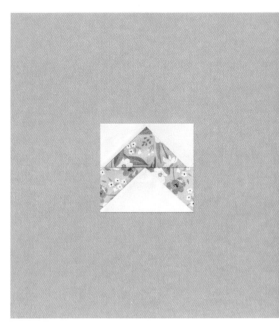

3 Sew a print flying geese unit to the top of a background flying geese unit. Press. Repeat to make a set of 4 chevron units.

4 Sew a 2½" background and a 2½" print square together. Press. Sew a 2½" x 4½" print rectangle to the bottom of the unit. Press.

5 Mark a diagonal line on the reverse side of (2) 2½" background squares. Place 2 marked squares atop a unit as shown. Sew on the marked line and trim the excess fabric. Press. Repeat to make a set of 4 corner units.

6 Arrange the set of 4 chevron units, 4 corner units, and a 4½" border fabric square in 3 rows of 3 as shown. Sew the units together in rows and press in opposite directions. Sew the rows together. Press. Make 20 blocks.

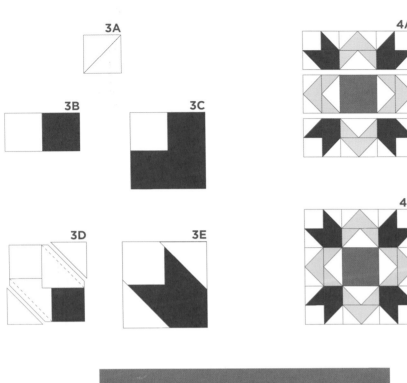

5 arrange & sew

Refer to the diagram below to layout the blocks in **5 rows of 4**. Sew the rows together and press the seams in opposite directions. Nest the seams and sew the rows together. Press.

6 inner border

From the inner border fabric, cut (6) 2½" strips across the width of the fabric. Sew the strips together to form 1 long strip. Trim the inner borders from this strip. Refer to Borders (pg. 118) in the Construction Basics to measure, cut, and attach the borders. The approximate lengths of the strips are 60½" for the sides and 52½" for the top and bottom.

7 outer border

From the outer border fabric, cut (7) 6" strips across the width of the fabric. Sew the strips together to form 1 long strip. Trim the outer borders from this strip. Refer to Borders (pg. 118) in the Construction Basics to measure, cut, and attach the borders. The approximate lengths of the strips are 64½" for the sides and 63½" for the top and bottom.

8 quilt & bind

Layer the quilt with batting and backing, then quilt. See Construction Basics (pg. 118) to finish your quilt.

Peace, Love, and Quilting
Sassy Spools Quilt

Welcome back, Missouri Star Family! We can't begin to express how excited we are to celebrate our 13th Birthday Bash with you, actually with you. Last year's Bash just wasn't the same without you or the town, so it's going to feel phenomenal to come together and quilt. And sew, and paint, and just create TOGETHER! "Come Together" is our theme this year, so we're having a little throwback to the era of peace, love, creativity, and kindness: The 1960s! It was such a pivotal and powerful decade for so many things: the Civil Rights movement, women's liberation, music, fashion, and technology. So as an homage to this year's theme and the 60s, we will all be donning tie-dye Birthday Bash T-shirts. Unlike bell bottoms, tie-dye isn't really making a comeback because it never left! We aren't kidding about the bell bottoms either, they really are back.

If you ever wore bell bottoms, tie-dye, or choker necklaces, you probably remember your parents' faces the first time you came down for breakfast wearing the "new style." Self-expression was so big during the '60s, from the way we decided to dress to the music we listened to. Who was your go-to band or musician when it came to tunes? There was so much great music being made, we had such a magical variety to choose from: The Beach Boys, The Beatles, Carole King, and Tina Turner! Did you hear about Tina Turner and

Carole King being second-time inductees into the Rock & Roll Hall of Fame this year? Two amazing female artists who wowed us with their talent in the '60s earning a spot in the Hall of Fame for a second time. How inspiring is that?

All right, all right, that's enough reminiscing as we're sure you're stoked to know what the 13th Birthday Bash is going to be like. Besides shopping, sewing, and dancing, we have a bunch of games and fab events lined up for you! On September 22nd, after you get checked in and settled, there will be Dinner with the Doans—all of them this time because Jenny and Ron's grandkids will be joining too! Between September 23rd and 25th, we'll all be having a blast with games, prizes, shaking our tailfeathers with Chuck the Duck, meeting some celebrity fabric designers, and there will also be a charity event for Project Linus!

So what do you think? Are you excited and ready to party? We hope so because if there's one thing we're looking forward to most about our 13th Birthday Bash, it's you—our Missouri Star family. Celebrating from afar last year just wasn't the same as having you here with us. We're more than ready to see you arrive in Quilt Town, USA, so we can smile, laugh, and create beautiful quilts and memories—together.

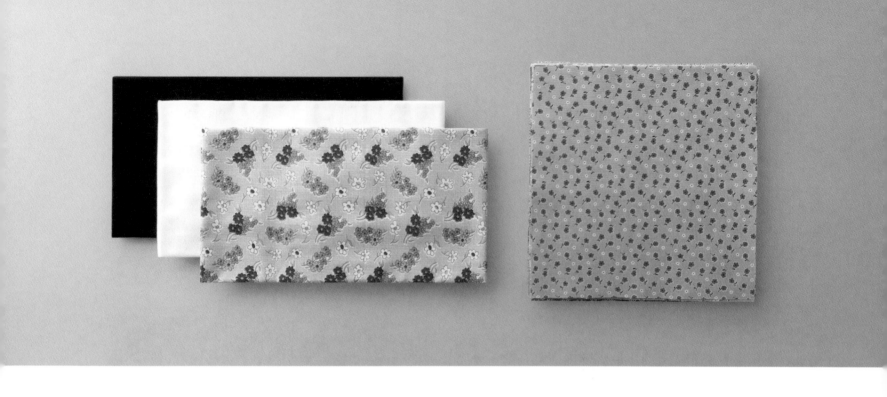

materials

QUILT SIZE
72½" x 81½"

BLOCK SIZE
10½" unfinished, 10" finished

QUILT TOP
1 package of 10" print squares
½ yard white solid fabric
1½ yards accent fabric
  - includes inner border

OUTER BORDER
1½ yards

BINDING
¾ yard

BACKING
5 yards - vertical seam(s)
  or 2½ yards of 108" wide

SAMPLE QUILT
Stitch by Lori Holt of Bee in my
  Bonnet for Riley Blake Designs

1 cut

From the package of 10" print squares:

- Select 7 squares and trim each to 10" x 7". Subcut a **total of (13)** 4½" x 7" rectangles.

- Select 7 squares and cut each in half vertically to yield a **total of (14)** 5" x 10" rectangles.

- Set the remaining squares aside for now.

From the white solid fabric, cut (4) 2½" strips across the width of the fabric. Subcut a **total of (13)** 2½" x 8½" rectangles and a **total of (13)** 2½" x 1½" rectangles from the strips.

From the accent fabric:

- Cut (13) 2½" strips across the width of the fabric.
  - From 4 strips, subcut (6) 2½" x 7" rectangles.

  - From 1 strip, cut (16) 2½" squares.

  - From 1 strip, subcut (2) 2½" x 7" rectangles and (10) 2½" squares resulting in a **total of (26)** 2½" x 7" rectangles and a **total of (26)** 2½" squares.

  - Set the 7 remaining strips aside for the inner border.

- Cut (10) 1½" strips across the width of the fabric.
  - From 6 strips, subcut (4) 1½" x 10" rectangles.

  - From 2 strips, subcut (12) 1½" x 3½" rectangles.

  - From 1 strip, subcut a **total of (26)** 1½" squares.

  - From 1 strip, subcut (2) 1½" x 10" rectangles and (2) 1½" x 3½" rectangles for a **total of (26)** 1½" x 10" rectangles and a **total of (26)** 1½" x 3½" rectangles.

2 make upper units

Sew a 1½" x 3½" accent rectangle to both sides of a 1½" x 2½" white solid rectangle. Press. **Make 13** upper units and set them aside for now. **2A**

3 make the bottom units

Mark a diagonal line corner to corner on the reverse side of each 2½" accent square. **3A**

Place a marked square on both ends of a 2½" x 8½" white solid rectangle. Sew on the marked lines and then trim the excess fabric ¼" from the sewn seam. Press. **Make 13** bottom units and set them aside for now. **3B 3C**

4 make the center units

Mark a diagonal line once corner to corner on the reverse side of each 1½" accent square. **4A**

Place a marked square on the top corners of a 4½" x 7" print rectangle. Sew on the marked lines and then trim the excess fabric ¼" from the sewn seam. Press. **4B 4C**

Sew a 2½" x 7" accent rectangle to both sides of the unit. Press. **Make 13** center units and set them aside for now. **4D**

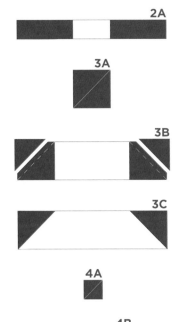

2A

3A

3B

3C

4A

4B

4C

1 Sew a 1½" x 2½" white solid rectangle between (2) 1½" x 3½" accent rectangles. Press to make an upper unit.

2 Lay (2) 2½" accent squares with a diagonal line marked on the reverse side on each end of a 2½" x 8½" white solid rectangle. Sew on the marked lines and trim off the excess fabric. Press to make a bottom unit.

3 Lay (2) 1½" accent squares with a diagonal line marked on the reverse side on the upper corners of a 4½" x 7" print rectangle. Sew on the marked lines and trim off the excess fabric. Press.

4 Sew a 2½" x 7" accent rectangle to both sides of the unit. Press.

5 Sew the unit you just created between the upper and bottom units you made previously. Press.

6 Sew a 1½" x 10" accent rectangle to both sides of the unit. Press.

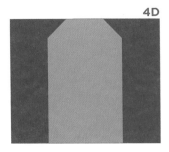

4D

5 block construction

Sew 1 upper unit to the top of a center unit. Press. Sew 1 bottom unit to the bottom. Press. **5A**

Sew a 1½" x 10" accent rectangle to both sides of the unit. Press. **Make 13**. Measure 5" from the center and trim each block to measure 10" wide. **5B**

Block Size: 10" unfinished, 9½" finished

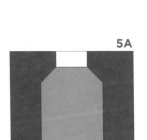

5A

6 arrange & sew

Select (22) 10" print squares from your package and set the rest aside for another project. Arrange the 10" print squares,

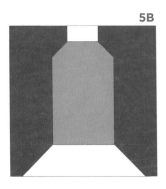

5B

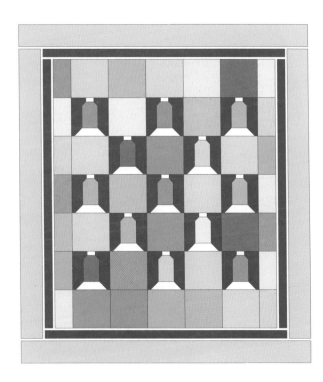

5" x 10" print rectangles, and completed blocks in **7 rows of 7** as shown in the diagram below. Sew together in rows and press. Sew the rows together and press to complete the quilt center.

7 inner border

Pick up the strips set aside and sew them together to form 1 long strip. Trim the inner borders from this strip. Refer to Borders (pg. 118) in the Construction Basics to measure, cut, and attach the borders. The approximate lengths of the strips are 67" for the sides and 61" for the top and bottom.

8 outer border

From the border fabric, cut (7) 6" strips across the width of the fabric. Sew the strips together to form 1 long strip. Trim the outer borders from this strip. Refer to Borders (pg. 118) in the Construction Basics to measure, cut, and attach the borders. The approximate lengths of the strips are 71" for the sides and 72" for the top and bottom.

9 quilt & bind

Layer the quilt with batting and backing, then quilt. See Construction Basics (pg. 118) to finish your quilt.

The Missouri Quilt Museum
World's Largest Spool of Thread Quilt

A visit to Quilt Town, U.S.A. just isn't complete without a tour of The Missouri Quilt Museum.

This incredible museum is housed in the old 30,000-square-foot Hamilton schoolhouse located at 300 East Bird St. in Hamilton, Missouri. Bit by bit, museum founders Ryan and Dakota Redford have remodeled the 100-year-old building into a beautiful monument to the art of quilting. So far, two thirds of the project has been finished and already there is plenty to see and do. When the transformation is complete, our little town will boast the biggest quilt museum in the entire country.

So, what's inside? I'm so glad you asked! The Missouri Quilt Museum is filled with all sorts of fun sewing memorabilia including antique sewing machines, vintage buttons, paper patterns, and a delightful collection of over 500 old-fashioned toy sewing machines. There are spinning wheels, antique irons, and the world's largest thimble collection. And just for fun, there's an exhibit celebrating the rich heritage of our beautiful town.

Now, the quilts. The museum hosts rotating quilt exhibits featuring local quilters and big-name designers alike. Best of all, The Missouri Quilt Museum is the permanent home of a collection of modern quilts from The National Quilt Museum. This collection boasts over 600 of the best modern quilts dating back to 1980. The quilts are rotated every three to four months, so you can see something wonderful and new every time you visit.

Before you leave, be sure to stop in front of the museum to snap a selfie with Aurifil's World's Largest Spool of Thread, a twenty-two-foot-tall spool wrapped with over one million yards of multi-colored thread. Visitors are invited to add a few yards of their own, so this spool just becomes more beautiful and interesting as time goes by.

Missouri Star Quilt Co. does not own the museum, but we sure love it, and we are grateful for the museum founders and sponsors like Aurifil for creating such a unique and wonderful destination right here in Hamilton, Missouri. This museum is an absolute treasure, and so many fun additions are in the works, including quilt-block flower gardens, a sewing-themed mini golf course and a cute playground with a "sewing machine" slide and swing set.

So, come to Hamilton, my friends! Visit the shops, meet the people, and don't forget to take a tour of The Missouri Quilt Museum. I guarantee it will be a trip to remember!

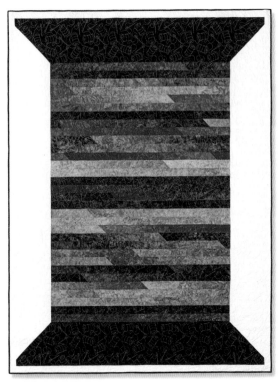

materials

QUILT SIZE
72½" x 91"

QUILT TOP
1 roll 2½" print strips
1½ yards accent fabric
2 yards background fabric
  - includes border

BINDING
¾ yard

BACKING
5½ yards - vertical seam(s)
  or 2¾ yards of 108" wide

SAMPLE QUILT
Artisan Batiks - Patina Handpaints
  by Lunn Studios for
  Robert Kaufman

World's Largest Spool
of Thread Quilt

1 cut

From the accent fabric, cut (4) 12" strips across the width of the fabric. From the background fabric, cut (5) 10" strips across the width of the fabric. From 1 strip, subcut (4) 10" squares. Set the remaining fabric aside.

2 make 1 long strip

Remove selvages from the ends of each print strip. Place the ends of (2) 2½" print strips at a right angle, right sides together. Mark a 45° diagonal line as shown. **2A**

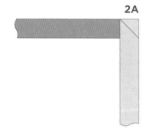

Sew on the drawn line. Trim the excess fabric ¼" away from the sewn seam. Press open. **2B 2C**

Continue in this manner to add all of the remaining strips on 45° diagonals to make 1 long strip. Cut 18" off the end of the strip. This ensures the triangles will not end up on the edge of the quilt center.

3 make the thread

Pick up both ends of the long strip. Lay 1 end on top of the other, right sides together. Sew the strip to itself lengthwise all the way back to the fold. Don't worry about twisting. When you are close to the end, cut the fold, undoing any twists, and finish sewing the 2 strips together.

Layer the ends of the 2-strip set right sides together and repeat sewing lengthwise. Cut the fold and finish sewing the 4-strip set. Continue sewing the strips together and cutting in this fashion 5 times until your strip set is a **total of 32** strips tall. Press. Trim the width of this thread unit to 50". **Note**: If your thread unit is less than 50", you will need to adjust the spool ends in the next section. Add 19" to the width of your thread unit for the spool end length.

4 make the spool ends

Sew the (4) 12" accent strips end-to end to create 1 long strip. Press. Trim (2) 12" x 69" rectangles from this strip. Mark a line from corner to corner once on the diagonal on the reverse side of each 10" background square. **4A**

Place a 10" marked background square on each lower corner of an accent rectangle, right sides facing. Notice that the angles of the marked lines are reflected. Sew on the marked lines. Trim the excess fabric away ¼" from the sewn seam line. Press open. **Make 2**. **4B 4C**

1 Remove selvages from the ends of all of the print strips. Place the ends of (2) 2½" print strips at a right angle, right sides together. Mark a 45° diagonal line as shown.

2 Sew on the drawn line. Trim the excess fabric ¼" away from the sewn seam.

3 Press open.

4 Mark a line from corner to corner once on the diagonal on the reverse side of each 10" background square.

5 Place a 10" marked background square on each lower corner of an accent rectangle, right sides facing. Notice that the angles of the marked lines are reflected. Sew on the marked lines. Trim the excess fabric away ¼" from the sewn seam line.

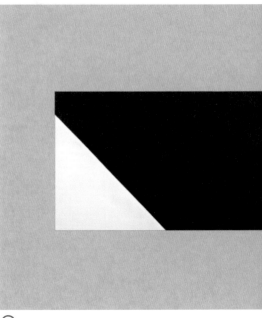

6 Press open.

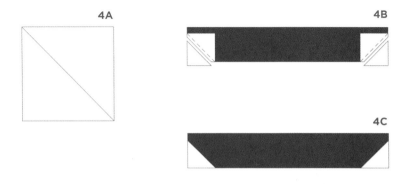

4A 4B 4C

5 arrange & sew

Sew the (4) 10" background strips end-to-end to create 1 long strip. Press. Trim (2) 10" x 64½" rectangles from this strip. Set the remaining piece aside for the border. Refer to the diagram on the left. Sew a 10" x 64½" background rectangle to either side of the thread unit and press.

Sew a spool end to the top and bottom of the large thread unit just made. Notice the spool units reflect. Press.

6 border

From the 10" piece set aside earlier, cut (4) 2½" strips across the width of the strip. Cut (5) 2½" strips across the width of the background fabric.

Sew all of the 2½" strips end-to-end to make 1 long strip. Trim the borders from this strip. Refer to Borders (pg. 118) in the Construction Basics to measure, cut, and attach the borders. The approximate lengths are 87½" for the sides and 73" for the top and bottom. **Note**: These lengths will be different if your thread unit was less than 50".

7 quilt & bind

Layer the quilt with batting and backing, then quilt. See Construction Basics (pg. 118) to finish your quilt.

Talavera Tile Sew-Along
PART 4

STUDIO STAR BLOCK SIZE
9½" unfinished, 9" finished

FANCY FLIGHT BLOCK SIZE
2½" x 4½" unfinished,
2" x 4" finished

BLOCK SUPPLIES - STUDIO STAR
(1) 10" fabric B square
(2) 10" fabric C squares
(1) 10" fabric D square
(1) 2½" fabric F strips
    (cut from yardage)
(4) 2½" fabric G strips
    (cut from yardage)

BLOCK SUPPLIES - FANCY FLIGHT
(1) 10" fabric B square
(2) 10" fabric D squares
(1) 10" fabric E square
(4) 2½" fabric G strips
    (cut from yardage)

Note: Fabric A is not used in Part 4.

QUILT SIZE
77" x 77"

WHOLE QUILT TOP
1 package 10" print squares
1 package of 10" Talavera Tile
squares:
  • 10 fabric A squares
  • 10 fabric B squares
  • 7 fabric C squares
  • 14 fabric D squares
  • 11 fabric E squares
¼ yard fabric B
  - includes Lemon Star border
¼ yard fabric C
1½ yards fabric F
  - includes sashing and
    Lemon Star border

3¼ yards fabric G
  - includes sashing,
    Lemon Star border, and binding

BINDING
¾ yard

BACKING
4¾ yards – vertical seam(s)
  or 2½ yards 108" wide *

*Note: 2 packages of 10" print squares can be substituted for the package of Talavera Tile squares. You will need a **total of (52)** 10" squares. Other packages of squares may not have the same number of duplicate prints needed to match the quilt exactly.*

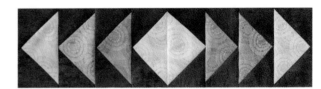

FANCY FLIGHT BLOCK

STUDIO STAR BLOCK

Fabric Key

A — Dark Royal
B — Teal
C — Seafoam
D — Sunshine
E — Orange
F — White
G — Navy

2A

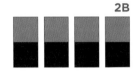

2B

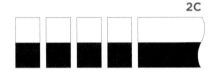

2C

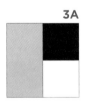

3A

3B

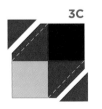

3C

3D

STUDIO STAR
1 cut

From 1 fabric B square, cut (4) 2½" strips across the square for a **total of (4)** 2½" x 10" fabric B rectangles.

From 2 fabric C squares, cut (4) 2½" strips across the width of each square. Subcut each strip into (2) 2½" x 4½" rectangles for a **total of (16)** 2½" x 4½" fabric C rectangles.

From 1 fabric D square, cut (1) 2½" strip across the width of the square. Subcut the strip into a **total of (4)** 2½" fabric D squares. Set the remaining fabric aside for the bonus project.

From the fabric F yardage, cut (1) 2½" strip across the width of the fabric.

From the fabric G yardage, cut (4) 2½" strips across the width of the fabric.

- Subcut 1 strip into a **total of (4)** 2½" x 10" fabric G rectangles.

- Subcut 2 strips into (16) 2½" squares for a **total of (32)** 2½" fabric G squares.

- Set the remaining strips aside for the moment.

2 sew 2-patch units

Pick up the 2½" x 10" fabric B and fabric G rectangles. Lay a fabric B rectangle right sides together with a fabric G rectangle and sew them together along 1 long edge. Open each strip set and press toward fabric G. **Make 4** strip sets. **2A**

Cut each strip set into 2½" increments to **make 16** B/G 2-patch units. **2B**

In a similar manner, sew the fabric F strip and fabric G strip together along 1 long edge. Open and press toward the darker fabric. Cut the strip set into 2½" increments to **make 16** F/G 2-patch units. **2C**

3 sew corner units

Sew a 2½" x 4½" fabric C rectangle to each F/G 2-patch unit as shown. **Make 16**. **3A**

Fold each of the 2½" fabric G squares on the diagonal, wrong sides facing. Press the crease in place. **3B**

Place a creased square on 2 corners of a unit as shown and sew each in place on the diagonal. Trim the excess fabric away ¼" from the sewn seam. Open and press. **Make 16** corner units. **3C 3D**

4 block construction

Pick up (1) 2½" fabric D square, 4 B/G 2-patch units, and 4 corner units. Layout the block in rows as shown. Rows 1 and 3 are made by placing a corner unit on either side of a B/G 2-patch unit. Be aware of the direction the 2-patch and corner units are placed. Sew the units together and press towards the 2-patch unit. **Make 2**. **4A**

Row 2 is made by sewing a B/G 2-patch unit to either side of the 2½" fabric D square. Sew the units together and press towards the 2-patch units. **4B**

Nest the seams and sew the 3 rows together. Press. **Make 4** Studio Star Blocks. **4C 4D**

Studio Star Block Size:
10½" unfinished, 10" finished

FANCY FLIGHT
1 cut & sort

Cut 1 fabric B, 2 fabric D, and 1 fabric E squares into (4) 2½" strips across the width of each square. Subcut each strip into (2) 2½" x 4½" rectangles. You will need a **total of (8)** 2½" x 4½" fabric B rectangles, a **total of (16)** 2½" x 4½" fabric D rectangles, and a **total of (8)** 2½" x 4½" fabric E rectangles.

From the fabric G yardage, cut (4) 2½" strips across the width of the fabric. Subcut each strip into (16) 2½" squares for a **total of 64**.

2 sew

Fold each of the fabric G squares once on the diagonal, wrong sides facing. Press the crease in place to use as your sewing line. **2A**

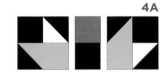
4A

4B

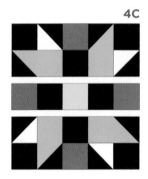
4C

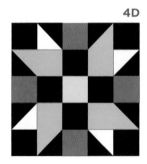
4D

2A

2B

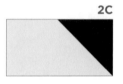
2C

2D

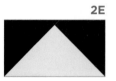
2E

3A

3B

Lay a creased square on top of a 2½" x 4½" rectangle, right sides together, as shown. Sew on the diagonal line. Trim the excess fabric ¼" from the seam. **2B**

Open and press toward the outside edge. **2C**

Lay a second creased square atop the opposite end of the 2½" x 4½" rectangle, right sides together, as shown. Sew on the creased line, then trim the excess fabric ¼" from the seam. **2D**

Open and press toward the outer edge. **2E**

Repeat with the remaining rectangles and creased squares to make a **total of 8** B blocks, a **total of 16** D blocks, and a **total of 8** E blocks.

Fancy Flight Block Size:
2½" x 4½" unfinished, 2" x 4" finished

3 arrange & sew

Lay out 1 B block, 2 D blocks, and 1 E block as shown. Sew the blocks together and press towards the left. **Make 8** half-rows. **3A**

Sew 2 half-rows together as shown and press the center seam to 1 side. **Make 4**. **3B**

Fancy Flight Row Size:
4½" x 16½" unfinished, 4" x 16" finished

Bound in Secrets and Lies

PART FOUR: TRUTH ON THE BIAS

a fiction novella, in six parts written by **Hillary Doan Sperry**

Mena stepped close, and Jenny couldn't tell if it was anger or fear in her eyes when she repeated her question. "Where did you hear the name Mish? No one is supposed to know about that."

The dark room felt smaller as Mena interrogated her. Jenny tried to think back. "During your meeting with Jed. But you're Mish, aren't you?"

Mena sneered. Jed had told her that Mish was someone to be afraid of, but from what she could tell Mena was just a bully.

"You can't keep doing this, trying to hurt Grace and ruin her business, all so you can take her house. That's not going to happen," Jenny said.

"You think this is all so I can take Grace's house?" Mena laughed, a cruel snap of sound. "I don't even like her house. I thought I did once, but I can barely stand living in this tiny town. All I want is to get out."

"So why are you doing this? Grace isn't hurting anyone." Mena laughed again. The mocking sound ran a trickle of fear

down Jenny's back. Jenny had been wrong. She didn't know about what, but it was obvious that Mena's plans weren't what Jenny had thought they were.

"Mena?" a man's voice called from somewhere else in the house. Mena clenched her jaw and glared at Jenny as she responded. "Yeah, Charlie? I'm here."

"I need help. Will you ..." He didn't finish, but the pain that had mixed in with Mena's anger and superiority gave Jenny the slightest pause of hesitation.

"Don't touch anything. I'll be right back." Mena crossed the room and disappeared down the hallway.

Jenny took several seconds, trying to decide if she should run straight for the door or try and get some answers out of this mixed-up woman. She looked around the room. Maybe she could get her answers without Mena at all.

Quilts were taking up most of the space in the tidy room. The walls were covered in floral artwork and rows of china cups.

Jenny's brow furrowed. It wasn't the lair of your typical villain. She walked over to the worn but clean sofa and looked at the quilt stacked on top of the pile. She ran a hand over the stitching and realized the one in process was Grace's missing quilt. She picked it up and started for the door. Answers could wait.

Hitching up the excess fabric as Jenny passed a chair, the fabric swung out hitting a lamp. It toppled from the table, crashing to the floor.

"What are you doing?" Mena appeared in the hall, her aggressive tone calling up Jenny's defenses. "I told you to stay there." Mena bolted across the floor, reaching to retrieve the quilt. Jenny gripped it, planting herself against the younger woman's intensity.

"This isn't yours," Jenny said, trying to keep it out of her grip.

"Of course it is. It's a family quilt on my husband's side. I tore it. That's why Jed gave me the linen. See?" She grabbed the edge where she was repairing the binding with a strip of white linen. It didn't make any sense; the white fabric was completely out of place.

"This is Grace's quilt. I know, she showed it to me a week ago." Jenny held tight, trying to be gentle but not letting go. Something crinkled like wrappers or paper inside the quilt. Then when Mena shifted her grip a folded paper slipped out of the binding.

It was thin like a receipt, and Mena dropped, snatching it up and tucking it into her pocket. In the process she released the quilt and Jenny was able to back up to the kitchen.

"Fine. Take it. If Grace is so desperate for a quilt that she'd steal my husband's heirloom, she can have it." Mena trembled, breathless and worried. This was not the vision of the evil mastermind set to kill Grace and steal her house that Jenny had imagined.

"I'm sorry, Mena. Can I just show Grace? If it's not hers I'll bring it back."

"Put it down, Mrs. Doan." Charlie stepped into their circle from the hallway, leaning on a cane, and his upper lip twisted in a sneer. He might still be recovering from a car accident, but as he stepped forward, he raised his cane and aimed it at her, letting it hover in the air. "You will kindly replace our belongings and leave this house. Mena may not be Mish, but I know who is, and he will not take kindly to you questioning and intimidating my family." Jenny's eyebrows rose. Mena wasn't Mish? She looked between them and set the quilt down. Charlie lowered his cane, but he didn't relax. He settled his weight onto the stick and kept his eyes glued to her every movement.

"I'm sorry for the misunderstanding." Jenny held her hands up and stepped back from the quilts to make it clear she wouldn't touch it again. "If there is anything you can share with me or tell me about what's going on, please do. I only want to help my friend."

Neither of them spoke for a moment, and then Mena stepped forward, taking the quilt. "If I was Mish, you'd be dead right now. Who do you think put Charlie in the hospital?"

Jenny pulled back. "I thought it was Jed. But he's not Mish."

Charlie rolled his eyes. "No. Jed's not Mish, he's just his puppet. So, yeah Jed crashed the car with me in it, but it was Mish's gun to Jed's head if he didn't. I don't blame Jed."

"Who do you blame?" Jenny asked, her whole body leaning in as if inches from her answer.

Charlie shook his head and lifted his cane again, this time pointing her to the door. "You need to go, and you need to be a lot more careful. I'd rather tomorrow's headline be 'New Animal Processing Plants' than a murder."

Jenny's throat went dry, and she nodded. She wasn't looking to die. She'd tell the police what she knew and leave the sleuthing to them.

* * *

After a long talk with Officer Wilkins and settling Grace in, Jenny found herself riding home in Cherry's red convertible. Bernie and Dotty had gone home hours before, and Jenny felt lucky that Cherry had still been around. But even that couldn't hide the fact that both the Reyeses and Jed had warned her about who was after Grace.

"I'm not sure what to do about all this." Jenny had found a spool of thread in the side pocket of Cherry's car and sat turning it anxiously, the gray purple color matching her mood. "Grace could die for nothing, and all I did was sit here and watch. How can you just sit here?"

"I'm not just sitting," Cherry said, sparing a glance as they drove past the food court patio with all its lights strung up and glowing in the dusky evening. Jenny nearly asked her to stop. But milkshakes wouldn't make it better so she watched it roll past.

Cherry continued, "Jenny, you saved Grace's life—twice! And confronting two of the people involved in a series of thefts and accidents is hardly sitting around. Granted that's you and not me, but I'm helping in the only way I know how. I'm sharing information with the police and keeping my eyes open for anything new. You did tell the police about the bricks and the fabric, right?"

Jenny scowled. "I did. And Wilkins gave me his she's-a-crazy-lady look."

"I don't think I've seen that one," Cherry said, fighting a smile. Jenny's lip twitched. "Maybe that's because you're not crazy."

Cherry giggled as they pulled into Jenny's driveway. "Well, I'm glad you talked to him."

"Me too," she said, remembering how he'd accepted the information without writing a single thing down. And that look.

"They really have no idea how big this is."

Cherry didn't have a chance to respond before Ron greeted them. Jenny was never more grateful to be wrapped in her husband's arms. "It's been an awful day."

"I wish you would have let me come get you," he said, still holding her after Cherry's car had disappeared down the road.

"You would have come in a second, wouldn't you?" Jenny tipped her head back to smile at the man she loved. "There was no need. Cherry was right there. I'm glad to know I have a knight in shining armor if I need one though."

Together they went inside, and Jenny filled Ron in on the details of what had happened that day.

"I can't believe all that really happened. You're sure Jed is clear?"

Ron stood as he made his way down to the kitchen.

"Clear is a strong word. He's made some bad choices, but I think Grace is right to hold off on turning him in. Sometimes the easy answer is so tempting. He doesn't want to do this, and if I keep working on him, I think he'll tell me who Mish is."

"Jenny, that's a really bad idea. You need to stay away from it. Tell the police to question Jed."

"Jed will never talk to them and you know it." Jenny stuck a needle into the binding of a quilt she was finishing for someone in New Jersey.

"That's not the point. You can't keep throwing yourself in the middle of things."

"If I don't, who will?"

"The police," Ron said matter-of-factly.

"They'll lock up Jed and not ask another question. There are too many things that he's done for them to see anyone else."

"Give them a chance."

Jenny's needle stilled, and she looked up at Ron. "Fine. I'll give them a chance, but they're searching for the wrong person."

Ron sighed. "Wilkins and Dunn are pretty smart."

Jenny hoped they would be smart enough to look past the actions of a trapped young man. A loud jingle sounded on the TV, and the Merkle Fabrication logo twirled onto the screen. "Is that another fabric company coming to town? I wonder if Missouri Star knows them."

Ron chuckled. "I doubt it. Unless they're getting into hog processing. Merkle Fabrication & Processing is a big animal farming conglomerate. They've been voted out of the county for years, but the last time through they were given permission if they could get enough land in some certain area."

"Farming? Why is that bad?" Jenny watched the images of happy people working in a factory and wondered what they were trying to sell.

"It's a farming group, but their business is animal processing. It creates a lot of waste and taints the land for other types of farming."

I'd rather tomorrow's headline be 'New Animal Processing Plants' than a murder. It seemed a little strange that Charlie would comment on the very organization moving into their county.

Ron scowled at the screen and turned toward the stairs as it changed to a news report on the price of quilt sales in recent auctions. "Now that's a market I can handle," he teased as he headed down the stairs. "You should be selling your quilts instead of teaching people to make them."

Jenny smiled but kept her eyes on the screen.

"Sales for some of the county's most beautiful art pieces are bringing a high price at auctions this month. Quilt prices are unusually high, reaching into the thousands for some quilts, but no one is complaining when market value brings better appreciation of the craft." The reporter disappeared from the screen.

Thousands of dollars? Jenny turned the spool of thread she'd been using on its side and spun it on the end table. It wasn't unheard of, but it was unusual. Worth every penny, she imagined, but definitely unusual. The camera panned the line of quilts as the auctioneer called out numbers and egged on the bidders. The quilt at the auctioneer's table was the very one she'd seen that afternoon. Grace's handmade pre-war heirloom quilt. The one that had supposedly been in Charlie's family for years.

Ron appeared at the head of the stairs. "I made cake. Here you go." He handed her a beautiful slice of chocolate cake, but it was the large scoop of vanilla ice cream that brought a smile to her face.

"You know me too well," she said, scooping a spoonful of ice cream into her mouth before testing the cake. She didn't love chocolate nearly as much as Ron, but using it as a vehicle to get ice cream to her lips made it a perfect evening treat.

Ron grinned and sat next to her, changing the station on the television. "Oh, and I brought up the mail earlier." He pulled it from the end table next to his side of the couch. "One of them looks like an actual letter. I thought you might enjoy opening that."

Jenny took the letters, setting her cake aside. She didn't recognize the handwriting on the note and there was oddly no postmark. People sometimes sent her letters with fun stories about quilting or how they had learned something new. They always lifted her mood. It had probably come through the customer service team and they dropped it in the mailbox since she'd been out of the office all day. She flipped the thick letter over and slid a finger under the flap, breaking the seal.

A corner of fabric stuck out of the envelope, and Jenny smiled. Someone had made her something. She pulled it out and gasped, dropping the deep red fabric in her lap. She brushed it off, one hand to her chest.

"What is it?" Ron asked, as his knight in shining armor training kicked in and he jumped up to retrieve the fabric. Then he dropped it. "It's wet." He shook his hand and wiped it against a napkin. "Is that blood?"

Jenny looked at him, unable to hide the worry on her face. "I don't know."

"Let me see that." Ron took the envelope from her. He pulled out a printed page marred with old blood stains that read: "Leave it alone. Or we will take care of you too." He looked up at her. "Jenny, I don't want you anywhere near Jed or that case. I don't want Grace to get hurt either but she's got people watching out for her. I want you so far away you can't hear it if the phone rings at her house."

Jenny frowned, but nodded. "That doesn't make sense, but I know what you mean. I'll tell the police about Jed in the morning."

And hopefully they would listen.

to be continued...

Mastering the
Lone Star

with Courtenay Hughes

The Lone Star pattern is one of the oldest recognizable quilt designs. It goes back centuries and it is known by many different names including the Star of Bethlehem, the Radiant Star, the Mathematical Star, the Star of the East, and many more. Another interesting aspect of Lone Star history is its significance as a treasured quilt pattern to Native American people. In many tribes they are simply called "Star quilts" or "Morning Star quilts" and the star design existed in their traditions long before they began making quilts.

The Morning Star was the name given to the planet Venus. When it appeared in the east just before the sunrise, it intrigued those who observed it. This bright star was thought to bring the light of day. The Morning Star has many symbolic meanings including hope, guidance, the inevitability of change and starting anew, protection, and especially in Native American culture, a connection between the spiritual and natural world as ancestors were seen as represented by stars in the sky.

In certain Native American traditions, gifting a Star quilt is a great honor to those who receive it and these treasured quilts are often presented to recipients who are at life's crossroads including births, coming of age ceremonies, graduations, weddings, anniversaries, and funerals. Giving a quilt to the relatives of someone who has passed on is a token of reverence for that person's life, a reminder of the path that the departed take to the stars, and a promise that they will be watched over by the Great Spirit.

The Lone Star quilt has long been revered by quilters around the world and we love it for so many reasons. It can be made with a different number of points, commonly six or eight (and sometimes even more), and in many different color combinations and block settings. With just the right color placement, the star practically glows from the center to the tips with brilliant color.

Because it is viewed as a challenging pattern, Lone Star quilt tops are often found unfinished in antique shops, and what a shame, because this intricate quilt design isn't as hard as you might imagine! With a few tips and tricks, this beautiful star block becomes a joy to assemble. It's truly a clever way of looking at strip piecing. Follow along as Courtenay Hughes teaches how to master the evasive Lone Star and make it one of your favorite quilt patterns—we promise!

We asked Courtenay, "What made you want to sew a Lone Star quilt?" She said, "As I was getting more confident in my quilt journey, I wanted to try the Lone Star. Quiltsmart came up with a foundation-pieced method to make a Lone Star, so I started with that method. I then moved on to strip pieced and paper pieced stars."

And Courtenay has learned a lot since that time! She said, "I learned that the Lone Star quilt has such an amazing history with Native American tribes. There are also many variations to this block—you can make one big Lone Star, a bunch of small ones, and many other variations. They are all so beautiful."

Deciding to create a Lone Star quilt can come with a lot of misconceptions, including the difficulty. They appear to be tricky because you are sewing on the bias, but Courtenay has come up with several tips and tricks to make those concerns go out the window!

Planning a Layout

To create the desired effect in your Lone Star quilt, plan your layout before you begin with a fabric chart. You can even use the Lone Star coloring page we've provided. It's very helpful to visualize how your colors will look together. Take your chart and tape a small piece of each fabric to it, labeling the pieces A-D.

Cutting Strips

You can definitely use a roll of 2½" strips, but you'll want to iron and starch them well first, testing one strip to see if it does shrink before you begin. Measure them to make sure they remain the same width and trim if necessary. But if you want really accurate results, the best plan of action is to use yardage, starch it well, and then cut your strips.

Sewing and Pressing

As you sew your strips together, choose a direction to press the seams and keep it consistent. Don't press your seams open as it will be a challenge to match up your points when you are piecing.

Piecing Stars

What if your seams don't match up perfectly? It can be tough to piece on the bias, but here's a handy trick: pin on the seam and also pin on either side of the seam intersection to keep it from shifting. Even if you never pin, now's the time!

Piecing the Background

You can choose to use a Y-seam here or split the background pieces in two, which is generally easier. Keep in mind that because your background piece will be split in two on the bias, it's important to make sure your fabric is starched well. Handle it carefully to avoid stretching it and always pin.

Norm and Nanette Quilt
by Elizabeth Hartman

Not too long ago, my friend Cherry and I decided to get together once a week and work on a project together. We started on this journey working on Elizabeth Hartman's cute Norm and Nanette gnome quilt. I can't even tell you how accomplished we felt putting all those sweet little gnomes together. It's not the typical kind of sewing I usually do. The entire block is pieced, from their pointy hats to their little boots. This pattern has been such a fun challenge for me! Plus, it's great to have a sewing buddy who keeps me going.

Antique Bow Tie Quilt

I am a quilt rescuer. I found this beautiful bow tie quilt top in an antique shop while I was traveling. The pattern intrigued me and I thought it would be perfect for precuts. After a thorough inspection, I decided it could be quilted. I know many of us are worried about finishing antique quilt tops, but I have found that it brings them new life and purpose.

We have an amazing variety of 1930s reproduction fabrics to choose from when I need to find a binding or make a repair. "Reproduction" means that these fabrics are new copies of fabrics that existed in the past so they represent that era perfectly and will blend beautifully with the antique fabrics in your quilt top. I was excited to find this blue floral print in our Mercantile shop to use for the binding, and just like that this quilt is ready for the second half of its life. I hope this inspires you and gives you courage to finish and use your antique quilt tops!

Chew On This
Skylight Quilt

When my kids were little, they were pretty boisterous. In fact, not much has changed since then! And it often proved difficult to keep seven kids calm when I needed a little peace and quiet around the house. That's when bubblegum came in handy. A sweet, stretchy hunk of gum could keep a rowdy child occupied for long enough for me to relax. Then, all the kids would have the "Biggest Bubble" competitions, splitting a package of gum between them to find out who was the bubble-blowing master! It was truly a sight to behold with those big, pink bubbles stuck to their little cheeks and noses. And just in case you were wondering, according to the Guinness Book of World Records, in 2004, Chad Fell of Double Springs, Alabama, blew the biggest bubble on record at 20 inches in diameter. He says the secret to success is using three pieces of Dubble Bubble gum.

The bubblicious story of Dubble Bubble gum begins in 1928 in Philadelphia, with a young man named Walter Diemer, an accountant for the Fleer Chewing Gum Company. When Diemer wasn't crunching numbers, he was experimenting with gum recipes of his own! After several failed attempts to make a more enjoyable, bubble-friendly gum, he finally concocted a formula less sticky and stretchier than other gums of that time. But the delicious gum that would later be named "Dubble Bubble" almost never came to be.

Just a day after Diemer's discovery, he misplaced the recipe and never found it again. Imagine it, we were almost denied one of the tastiest chewing gums ever! Obviously we avoided such a tragedy, and it was due to Diemer's determination; he spent the next few months experimenting until he recreated the recipe again. To test his bubble gum (before he lost it again), Diemer took about 100 samples to a local store and sold it for just a penny each. Guess what? It all sold out in a day! Dubble Bubble was an immediate success.

Here's one last thing to chew on, why pink? We're certainly not complaining—bubble gum pink is a scrumptious color, especially on fabric! But is there a reason why the standard shade for bubble gum is pink? Apparently so! It turns out Dubble Bubble didn't look as yummy as it tasted—as Diemer continued to perfect it, it always came out in a funky gray color. He decided to do a color test with red food dye, as it was the only shade of food coloring the Fleer Company had, and after diluting the red a bit he got a lovely, delicious shade of pink! The color was so appealing, it's been the standard bubble gum shade ever since. Good thing too because gray bubbles don't sound as fun or pretty as pink bubbles.

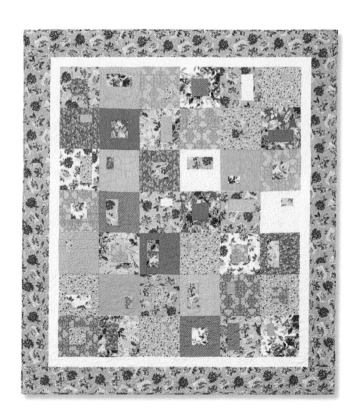

materials

QUILT SIZE
66" x 74½"

BLOCK SIZE
9" unfinished, 8½" finished

QUILT TOP
1 package of 10" print squares

INNER BORDER
½ yard

OUTER BORDER
1¼ yards

BINDING
¾ yard

BACKING
4¾ yards - vertical seam(s)
   or 2½ yards of 108" wide

SAMPLE QUILT
Lucy Jane by Lila Tuller
   for Riley Blake

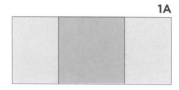

1A

1B

1 make A blocks

Choose 14 different 10″ print squares. Cut (1) 4″ strip and (2) 3″ strips across the width of each selected square. Subcut the 4″ strip into (1) 4″ square and (2) 4″ x 3″ rectangles. Subcut each 3″ strip into (1) 3″ x 9″ rectangle. Keep all matching pieces together.

Select 2 sets of pieces with different prints. Swap the 4″ squares. Sew a 4″ x 3″ rectangle to either side of the square as shown. Press. **1A**

Sew a 3″ x 9″ rectangle to the top and bottom of the unit. Press. **Make 14**. **1B**

A Block Size: 9″ unfinished, 8½″ finished

2 make B & C blocks

From each remaining 10″ print square, cut (1) 2″ strip, (1) 3″ strip, and (1) 5″ strip across the width of the square. Subcut the 3″ strip into (2) 3″ x 2″ rectangles and (1) 3″ x 6″ rectangle. Subcut each 2″ strip into a 2″ x 9″ rectangle. Subcut each 5″ strip into a 5″ x 9″ rectangle. Keep all matching rectangles together.

Select 2 sets of rectangles with different prints. Swap the 3″ x 6″ rectangles. Sew a 3″ x 2″ rectangle to either side of the 3″ x 6″ rectangle as shown. Press. **2A**

Sew the 2″ x 9″ rectangle to the top and the 5″ x 9″ rectangle to the bottom of the unit. Press. **Make 14** B blocks. **2B**

B Block Size: 9″ unfinished, 8½″ finished

Select 2 sets of rectangles with different prints. This time, swap (1) 3″ x 2″ rectangle from each set. Sew the matching 3″ x 2″ and 3″ x 6″ rectangles to the ends of the swapped 3″ x 2″ rectangle as shown. Press. **2C**

Sew the 2″ x 9″ rectangle to the top and the 6″ x 9″ rectangle to the bottom of the unit. Press. **Make 14** C blocks. **2D**

C Block Size: 9″ unfinished, 8½″ finished

2A

2C

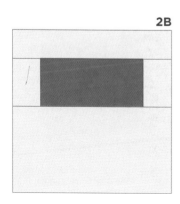

2B

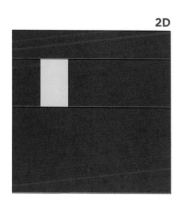

2D

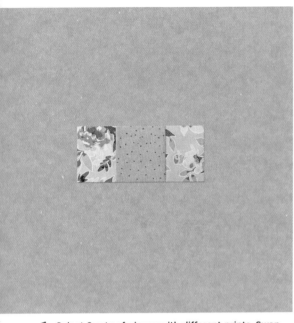

1 Select 2 sets of pieces with different prints. Swap the 4" squares. Sew a 4" x 3" rectangle to either side of the square as shown. Press.

2 Sew a 3" x 9" rectangle to the top and bottom of the unit. Press.

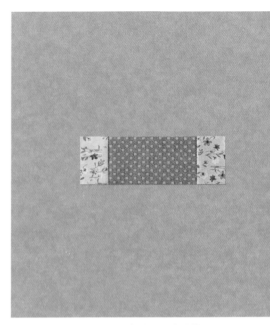

3 Select 2 sets of rectangles with different prints. Swap the 3" x 6" rectangles. Sew a 3" x 2" rectangle to either side of the 3" x 6" rectangle as shown. Press.

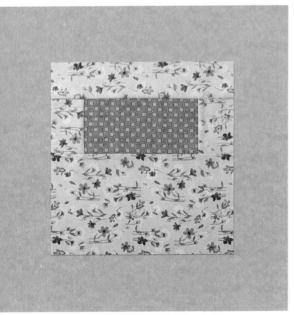

4 Sew the 2" x 9" rectangle to the top and the 5" x 9" rectangle to the bottom of the unit. Press.

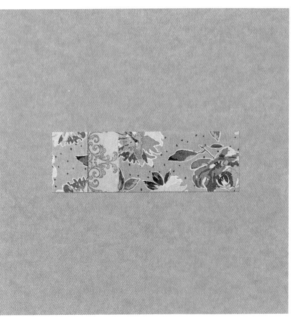

5 Select 2 sets of rectangles with different prints. Swap (1) 3" x 2" rectangle from each set. Sew the matching 3" x 2" and 3" x 6" rectangles to the ends of the swapped 3" x 2" rectangle as shown.

6 Sew the 2" x 9" rectangle to the top and the 6" x 9" rectangle to the bottom of the unit. Press.

3 arrange & sew

Refer to the diagram on the left to lay out your units in **7 rows of 6 blocks**. Pay close attention to the placement and orientation of the different blocks. Sew the blocks together in rows. Press the rows in opposite directions. Nest the seams and sew the rows together. Press.

4 inner border

Cut (6) 2½" strips across the width of the inner border fabric. Sew the strips together to make 1 long strip. Trim the inner borders from this strip. Refer to Borders (pg. 118) in the Construction Basics to measure, cut, and attach the borders. The approximate lengths are 60" for the sides and 55½" for the top and bottom.

5 outer border

Cut (7) 6" strips across the width of the outer border fabric. Sew the strips together to make 1 long strip. Trim the borders from this strip. Refer to Borders (pg. 118) in the Construction Basics to measure, cut, and attach the outer borders. The approximate lengths are 64" for the sides and 66½" for the top and bottom.

6 quilt & bind

Layer the quilt with batting and backing, then quilt. After the quilting is complete, see Construction Basics (pg. 118) to finish your quilt.

Quilting Is In Her DNA

Summer Squares Quilt

by Detra Braymen, a customer story

My love and passion for needlecraft and sewing goes back at least fifty-five years. My maternal grandmother taught me hand embroidery and crewel as soon as I could guide a needle, and I remember fondly taking sewing projects to the county fair. I started my first quilt when I was 16 and, even though I have yet to finish it, I still have it. What a long way I have come and now with the addition of precuts and breathtaking fabric lines, quilting has become my life!

My first trip to Missouri Star came when my local quilt shop asked me if I would like to come with a group and meet Jenny! At the time, I knew very little about Missouri Star, but of course said, "Sure!" I called a friend to come with me, and we headed to Hamilton. The minute I stepped foot in Hamilton, I knew it was a magical place. I was hooked! The shops, the people, the products, the vast knowledge and wisdom, the food … it just doesn't get any better.

I knew I just had to come to a retreat and signed up right away. We are still retreating as a group and come back annually to reconnect and reunite. I had a fantastic time but few in my group knew what I was dealing with on the back burner: I was adopted at birth, and had just received my DNA tests and was starting to piece together what turned out to be larger and more intricate than any quilt design that I had ever put together.

I had just gotten home and, when I thought I had put together all the missing links, I had to make the decision of whom to contact, and how to write that first letter.

Would they accept me? Would they be interested in me or would we have anything in common? Thanks to my daughter, we found who I believed was my aunt on social media. Once I saw her gorgeous quilt on her profile, and saw she used fabric from Me and My Sister Designs, I just knew she was the one to contact! I suddenly felt an indescribable peace come over me.

After 58 years of not knowing, I now have a new family! Unfortunately, it saddens me that my mother died of cancer in 2011, but I met my aunts and uncles, and even my great-uncle and great-aunt. I have met my maternal half-siblings and a handful of cousins and continue to have a close relationship with all of them! My aunt, Marla, lives in Iowa like me, although across the state. She is also an avid quilter like her mother (my grandma). We like the same patterns, the same fabrics, and finish each other's thoughts and sentences. We share the same values, humor, and even looks! She is just 18 months older than me, as my biological mother was the eldest. We have quilted together, been quilt shopping together, and spent last summer on a quilt trip to Sisters, Oregon, to see the Outdoor Quilt Show. We visit online almost daily, share our achievements, show our purchases, talk about frustrations, and seek opinions.

My hope and goal is that my aunt and I can come to Missouri Star to go on a retreat together soon. The discussion of how "nature vs. nurture" shapes us continues on and even though I had the very best life growing up, I can attest that we are related for a reason!

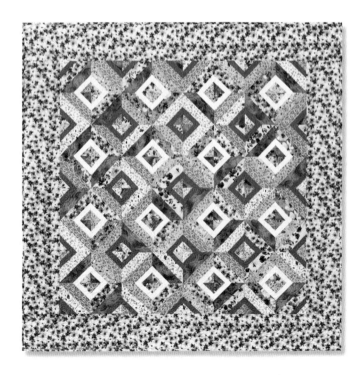

materials

QUILT SIZE
67" x 67"

BLOCK SIZE
7" unfinished, 6½" finished

QUILT TOP
1 roll of 2½" print strips
½ yard of gray fabric
½ yard of white fabric

BORDER
1½ yards

BINDING
¾ yard

BACKING
4¼ yards – vertical seam(s)
    or 2¼ yards of 108" wide

OTHER
Clearly Perfect Slotted
    Trimmer B
Spray starch - recommended

SAMPLE QUILT
Awakenings by Stephanie Ryan
    for Wilminton Prints
Kona Cotton - White
    for Robert Kaufman
Bella Solids - Graphite
    for Moda Fabrics

1A

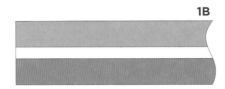

1B

2A

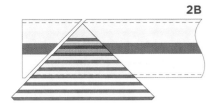

2B

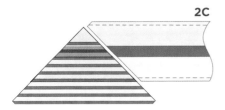

2C

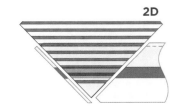

2D

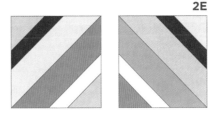

2E

1 make the strip sets

From both the gray and white fabrics, cut (10) 1½" strips across the width of each fabric.

Tip: The strip sets made in the next step will be cut on the bias. It is helpful to starch them while pressing.

Sew a print strip to either side of a 1½" gray strip as shown. Press. **Make 10** gray strip sets. **1A**

In the same manner, sew a print strip to either side of a 1½" white strip as shown. Press. **Make 10** white strip sets. **1B**

2 block construction

Lay a gray strip set atop a white strip set, right sides facing. Sew along both long edges creating a tube. **2A**

Lay the trimmer atop the sewn strip sets, along the left edge, and line the 7" mark of the trimmer with the bottom seam line. Cut along the left side. **2B**

Remove the triangle just trimmed. Cut along the right side of the ruler. **2C**

Set the triangle just cut aside for the moment. Turn the trimmer 180°, lay it along the left edge, and line the 7" mark of the trimmer with the top seam line. Trim the small strip away from the left edge, then cut along the right edge to create another triangle. **2D**

Repeat to cut 7 triangles from the sewn strip sets. **Note**: Each time the trimmer is lined up with the top edge, the small strip will be trimmed away from the left edge. Open and press each block. Repeat with the remaining strip sets to **make 64** blocks. **2E**

Block Size: 7" unfinished, 6½" finished

3 make the diamond units

Arrange 4 different blocks in a 4-patch formation as shown. Notice that the white strips create a center diamond. Sew the blocks together in 2 rows. Press in opposite directions. **3A**

Nest the seams and sew the blocks together. Press. **Make 16**. **3B**

1 Sew a 2½" strip to either side of a 1½" gray strip as shown. Press. Make 10 gray strip sets. In the same manner, sew a 2½" strip to either side of a 1½" white strip as shown. Press. Make 10 white strip sets.

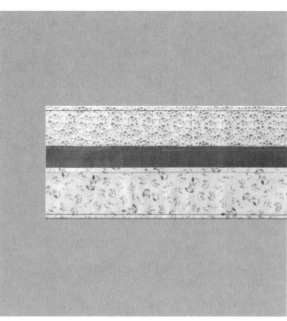

2 Lay a gray strip set atop a white strip set, right sides facing. Sew along both long edges creating a tube.

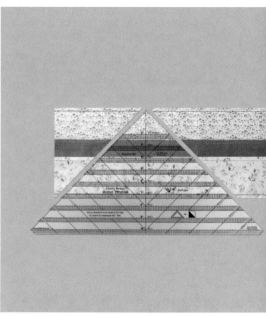

3 Lay the trimmer atop the sewn strip sets, along the left edge, and line the 7" mark of the trimmer with the bottom seam line. Cut along the left side. Move the triangle just trimmed out of the way and cut along the right side of the ruler.

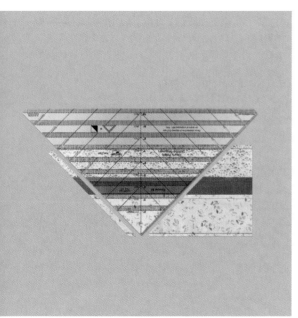

4 Turn the trimmer 180°, lay it along the left edge, and line the 7" mark of the trimmer with the top seam line. Trim the small strip away from the left edge, then cut along the right edge to create another triangle.

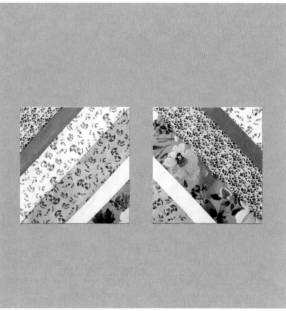

5 Open and press each block. Repeat with the remaining strip sets to make 64 blocks.

6 Arrange 4 different blocks in a 4-patch formation as shown. Notice that the white strips create a center diamond. Sew the blocks together in 2 rows. Press in opposite directions. Nest the seams and sew the blocks together. Press. Make 16.

3A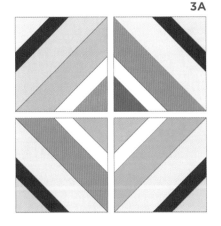

3B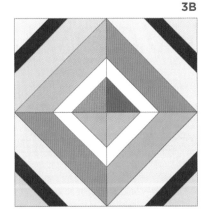

4 arrange & sew

Refer to the diagram on the left as necessary to lay out your units in **4 rows of 4**. Sew the units together in rows. Press the rows in opposite directions. Nest the seams and sew the rows together. Press.

5 border

Cut (6) 8″ strips across the width of the border fabric. Sew the strips together to make 1 long strip. Trim the borders from this strip. Refer to Borders (pg. 118) in the Construction Basics to measure, cut, and attach the borders. The approximate lengths are 52½″ for the sides and 67½″ for the top and bottom.

6 quilt & bind

Layer the quilt with batting and backing, then quilt. After the quilting is complete, see Construction Basics (pg. 118) to finish your quilt.

Mahota: Weaving Together Generations

Mahota Textiles is a unique company that produces "meaningful textiles that elevate the beauty and treasured culture" of their Southeastern heritage. They are the first textile company created and owned by a North American tribe. Weaving together generations, Mahota creates gorgeous blankets and fabrics that are filled with meaningful symbols and imagery brought to life in soft, warm wovens.

Honoring five generations of indigenous women, the logo for Mahota Textiles is a representation of early Native American symbols that have been discovered on shell carvings and pottery. It features five irregular concentric circles, as circles represent life, growth, and eternity in Chickasaw culture. This logo represents the five generations that have gone into creating their brand, ever expanding outward, continuing the legacy of Mahota.

"We're makers of art, of story, the threads that connect the inspiration of our ancestors to all of us in a modern world. These tell our stories; these create our brand."
— *Margaret Roach Wheeler, Founder*

photography courtesy of Mahota Textiles

photography courtesy of Mahota Textiles

The Mahota legacy begins long ago, in 1736. During a skirmish between the French and the Chickasaws, a young French girl living in the Southeast was kidnapped. Historical accounts vary, but one version says that she was picked up by a young warrior who spared her life after her own people were practically destroyed—the same warrior she would eventually marry. She was raised by an older woman in the Chickasaw tribe and eventually she became the bride of the warrior named Alikuhlo Hosh "the hummingbird" and they named a daughter "Mahota," which means "to separate by hand" in the Chickasaw and Choctaw languages. The name was given in honor of the beautiful works of art created by women in these Southeastern tribes. The French girl, who came to be known as "French Nancy" went on to be the mother of many children and was honored and loved by the Chickasaw people. She lived to an old age and, nearly three centuries later, the legend of French Nancy continues on.

Margaret Roach Wheeler, the founder of Mahota Textiles, is a Chickasaw textile designer, painter, sculptor, Native historian, and award-winning weaver. Margaret seeks to honor the spirit of creative Chickasaw women in her lineage including Mahota, Nancy Mahota, her grandmother, Juel, and her mother, Rubey. This lineage spans three centuries of Native American history.

Early on, she began her business creating handwoven fashion and creative textiles. Today she continues her art by mentoring other weavers, selling her own original handwoven textiles, designing for Mahota Textiles, and collaborating with the Chickasaw Nation. She is a part of the Mahota legacy, continuing centuries of craftsmanship that have been handed down through generations of indigenous makers.

We learned about Mahota Textiles when they reached out to us to help them create custom quilts out of their woven blanket remnants. We take the woven remnants, add batting and backing, and stitch the layers together to make thick, cozy quilts exclusively for their brand. These lovely quilts have themed patterns that go along with the blanket designs. For example, the "To Carry Sweet Things" quilt features one of our popular quilting patterns called "Sticky Buns" that looks like cinnamon buns with icing and the "Eagle" quilt features a quilting pattern called "Wind Swirls."

The "To Carry Sweet Things" quilt is named in honor of sweetgrass, the most fragrant of sacred Native American medicinal plants. It grows near streams and in meadows, abundant with tulip-shaped flowers that bloom in the spring. The aromatic grasses are then harvested in the summer. After it is cut, the sweetgrass is braided and dried to be used for medicinal tea, burned in cleansing ceremonies, and woven into baskets.

The "Eagle" quilt is named to revere this majestic bird that Southeastern tribes view as a symbol of strength, power, wisdom, and honor. Eagles are thought to be the strongest and bravest of all birds, the ones that fly the closest to the heavens. Eagle feathers are given to warriors for acts of bravery and bestowed in naming and religious ceremonies, as they are considered sacred.

Historically, everything created by the matrilineal societies of these Southeastern tribes was made with great care and love. Even tools were created to be aesthetically pleasing as they believed that the objects made with these tools would then be imbued with beauty and power. The same care goes into creating Mahota textiles. Created from a place of deep respect and admiration for their heritage, they seem to have a greater power to give comfort and express love—as do all quilts and blankets made from the heart.

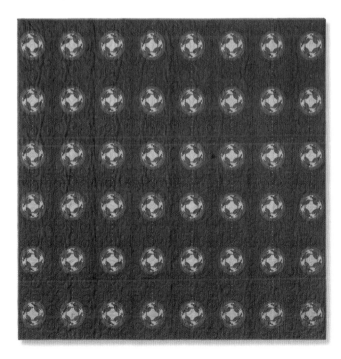

Summer Stargazing
60 Degree Stars Quilt

There's nothing better to do on a warm summer's night than going out to look at the stars! Out in the country and away from the city lights, we get quite the spectacular show on cloudless nights. Around sundown, I'll take a quilt out on the porch or into the backyard, lay down, and watch the cosmos dance above me. As the sun sets in its twilight hues, the stars blink into view one by one until they're uncountable! It really is the best way to spend an evening outside.

Stargazing is one of mankind's oldest pastimes. Every person who's ever lived, from us today, to the Founding Fathers, to the famous Renaissance painters, to the ancient Greeks, and even further into ancient history (and even prehistory!), has taken a moment to pause and look up at the heavens to see what they could see in the night sky. You can feel that connection to history whenever you look up and see one of the many ancient constellations that people from centuries past identified and wrote down.

The late summer sky is one of the best for stargazing. Some of the brightest stars in the sky are on display and, on top of the beautiful view, it's often nice enough to stay outside well into the night (as long as you pack the bug spray, that is!). I like to orient myself by finding the most recognizable constellation, the Big Dipper. Once I've found that, I can let my eyes wander and find the other constellations. I particularly like Cygnus the Swan (which you can find at the eastern point of the Summer Triangle of 3 bright stars), and its neighbor, the tiny dolphin Delphinus.

Besides the stars, if you're lucky, you can also see one of the most magical astronomical events: a shooting star! These tiny pieces of space rock whizz across the sky and burn up in an instant, but you'll remember seeing them forever. People think that these streaks of light are rare, but, if you spend a long time looking at the sky, you're likely to see one or two an hour. Sometimes, though, there can be a lot more! In fact, on the 12th and 13th of August, the Perseid meteor shower will light up the sky with up to 100 meteors per hour! After sunset, just look to the northeast, and you'll be able to make as many wishes as you want as the shooting stars rain down.

What are some of your favorite things in the night sky? Have you ever taken inspiration from the cosmos for a quilt? Tell us your stories on our Facebook page or write to us at **blockstories@misssouriquiltco.com**.

materials

QUILT SIZE
75" x 85"

BLOCK SIZE
8⅜" x 19⅛" unfinished
   half-hexagon,
7⅞" x 18¼" finished half-hexagon

QUILT TOP
1 roll of 2½" print strips
4¾ yards of background fabric
   - includes inner border

OUTER BORDER
1½ yards

BINDING
¾ yard

BACKING
5¼ yards – vertical seam(s)
   or 2¾ yards of 108" wide

OTHER
Missouri Star 8" Equilateral
   60 Degree Triangle Ruler
Spray starch - recommended

SAMPLE QUILT
**Wilmington Essentials
- Bubble Up** by Wilmington
   Prints

2A

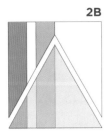

2B

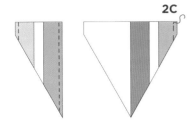

2C

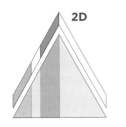

2D

2E   **2F**

1 cut

From the background fabric, cut (2) 9″ strips, (20) 5½″ strips, and (27) 1½″ strips across the width of the fabric. Set the 9″ strips aside for section 3 and (7) 1½″ strips aside for the inner border. You'll use the remaining (20) 1½″ strips and (20) 5½″ strips in the next section.

2 block construction

Tip: Since the strip sets made in the next step will later be cut on the bias, it is helpful to starch them while pressing. Sew a 5½″ background strip, a print strip, a 1½″ background strip, and another print strip together lengthwise in that order. Press. Cut the strip set into (3) 10″ segments. Set the remainder of the strip set aside for another project. **2A**

Lay 1 strip segment on your cutting surface with the print strips on the left side. Lay the ruler atop the segment and line up the center seam with the ruler center. Cut along the top sides of the ruler. You can cut slightly past the top point of the triangle, but do not cut all the way to the end of the fabric. Set this triangle A aside for the moment. **2B**

Fold the remainder of the segment in half along the short seam. Sew along the long edge. Remove the stitches on the short seam, open, and press. **2C**

Turn the unit 180° and use the ruler to cut another triangle as before. Notice the prints on this triangle B are in the opposite order of triangle A. **2D**

Repeat to cut triangles A and B from each of the remaining strip squares for a **total of 3** each.

Lay a triangle A as shown. **2E**

Lay a triangle B atop triangle A as shown, right sides facing, and matching the edges. Sew along the right edge. Open and press. **2F 2G**

Tip: Be careful not to stretch the triangle units while sewing. Starch again as needed. Lay a triangle A along the right edge of the unit as shown. Sew along the right edge. Open and press. **2H 2I**

Block Size: 8⅜″ x 19⅛″ unfinished half-hexagon, 7⅞″ x 18¼″ finished half-hexagon

Repeat to make a second block, beginning with a triangle B, then triangle A, followed by triangle B. **2J**

Keep the matching pairs of blocks together. **Make 20** block pairs.

1 Sew a 5½" background strip, a print strip, a 1½" background strip, and another print strip together lengthwise in that order. Press. Cut the strip set into (3) 10" segments. Set the remainder of the strip set aside for another project.

2 Lay 1 strip segment on your cutting surface with the prints on the left side. Line up the ruler center with the center seam. Cut along the top sides of the ruler. Do not cut all the way to the end of the fabric. Set this triangle A aside for the moment.

3 Fold the remainder of the segment in half along the short seam. Sew along the long edge. Remove the stitches on the short seam, open, and press.

4 Turn the unit 180° and use the ruler to cut another triangle as before. Notice the prints on this triangle B are in the opposite order of triangle A.

5 Lay a triangle A as shown. Lay a triangle B atop triangle A as shown, right sides facing, and matching the edges. Sew along the right edge. Open and press.

6 Lay a triangle A along the right edge of the unit as shown. Sew along the right edge. Open and press.

2G

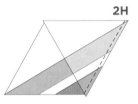

2H

2I

2J

3 arrange & sew

From the 9" background strips set aside earlier, use the ruler to cut 8 triangles. Cut each triangle in half.

Refer to the diagram below to arrange your blocks in **8 vertical rows of 5 blocks** each. Notice that matching blocks are in adjacent columns. 2 pairs of matching blocks will be split between the first and last columns. Sew the blocks in columns. Add a half triangle to the top and bottom of each column as shown.

4 inner border

Take the 1½" background strips set aside earlier and sew them together to make 1 long strip. Trim the borders from this strip. Refer to Borders (pg. 118) in the Construction Basics to measure, cut, and attach the borders. **Note**: The top and bottom inner borders are sewn on first. The approximate lengths are 63½" for the top and bottom and 75½" for the sides.

5 outer border

Cut (8) 5½" strips across the width of the outer border fabric. Set the remaining fabric aside for the bonus pieced backing. Sew the strips together to make 1 long strip. Trim the borders from this strip. Refer to Borders (pg. 118) in the Construction Basics to measure, cut, and attach the borders. The approximate lengths are 75½" for the sides and 75½" for the top and bottom.

6 quilt & bind

Layer the quilt with batting and backing, then quilt. After the quilting is complete, see Construction Basics (pg. 118) to finish your quilt.

Feathered Friends
Winter Cardinal Table Runner

I love keeping an eye on my bird feeders to see all the feathered friends who visit my yard! While I'm gardening, I like to get out in the yard and admire the birds that flock to the feeder for a quick snack. Even on cold days when I'm likely to stay indoors, I often spot the occasional bird visiting the feeder from the comfort of my kitchen window. The colorful birds are always the most exciting to spot, especially when I catch a beautiful red cardinal perched around the seed dispenser.

Cardinals are easier to spot during their mating season between the summer months of May through August, but cardinals are most commonly thought of during the winter months. Perhaps it's because they stand out so starkly against the white snow. Red Northern Cardinals are a seasonal symbol often used in home decor to create a festive holiday mood. So, why are these majestic red birds associated with winter holidays? Is it only their color?

According to old legends, cardinals symbolize beauty and warmth around the cold winter months, largely due to their bold red feathers. Spotting a Red Northern Cardinal is said to inspire people and spread joy and hope when the weather outside is frightfully grey. Others believe cardinals are good luck. Some even believe that the appearance of a cardinal represents the presence of an angel or loved one that has recently moved on.

With these beliefs in mind, it's no wonder people display cardinal decorations in and around their homes during the holiday season. Perhaps they bring happy memories of loved ones and comfort in thinking someone is watching over the household as they go about their holiday traditions. Or perhaps they instill a sense of warmth, hope, joy, even a bit of luck. Or maybe they're just simply beautiful to look at. In any case, they've become synonymous with the holidays.

Cardinals are instantly recognized by their brilliant red color, but not all cardinals are actually red. Even the Northern Red Cardinals, famously dressed in crimson, aren't completely red head to toe. The males get their vibrant color from the food they ingest, whereas most females have red chests and tan feathers. When a male cardinal eats more carotenoids in his diet, which are red pigments found in plants and berries, his feathers become a deeper red. The males and females can also be distinguished by their beaks, as males have red beaks and females have orange.

However, there are also several subspecies of cardinals in different colors. One of the rarest cardinal breeds is a yellow color. Albino cardinals are also out there, but scarcely seen. Birdwatchers have captured some beautiful stills of these feathered friends. Go ahead, search "rare cardinal breeds" online. The images will not disappoint!

Appearances aside, cardinals are talented creatures. Their singing puts windchimes to shame. The males sing a bellicose tune to attract a mate or ward off intruders, and the females sing melodious songs to let the males know they are hungry. Fun fact: these birds live up to 15 years and mate for life.

It's no surprise that these lovely creatures are the inspiration behind this beautiful table runner project. It'll make a charming accent to your holiday home decor. These majestic animals are sure to make your home feel more welcoming, festive, and cheery just in time for Christmas.

materials

PROJECT SIZE
64" x 16"

BLOCK SIZES
12½" unfinished, 12" finished

PROJECT TOP
1 yard red ombré fabric
½ yard green ombré fabric
 - includes border
2" x 4" rectangle black fabric scrap
¾ yard background fabric

BINDING
½ yard

BACKING
1½ yards - vertical seam(s)

OTHER
Clearly Perfect Slotted Trimmer - A

SAMPLE PROJECT
**Gelato - Ombré Red and
Ombré Green** by Maywood Studio

Grunge Basics - White Paper by
BasicGrey for Moda Fabrics

BONUS *Find the king size
quilt size in your
digital issue!*

94

2A

2B

2C

2D

1 cut

Note: Stack and label the like units as you cut.

From the red fabric, cut:
- (1) 3½" strip along the **length** of the fabric. Subcut (2) 3½" x 8½" rectangles and (2) 3½" x 6½" rectangles.

- (1) 4½" strip across the **width** of the fabric. Subcut (1) 4½" square. From the lightest part of the fabric, subcut (1) 4½" x 4" rectangle. Trim the rectangle to 4" square. Set the remaining fabric aside for another project.

- (2) 3" strips across the **width** of the fabric.
  ◦ Subcut 1 strip into (12) 3" squares.

  ◦ Subcut 1 strip into (4) 3" squares.

  ◦ Trim the remainder of the strip across the **width** creating (2) 1½" strips. Subcut a **total of (16)** 1½" squares.

- (2) 2½" strips across the **width** of the fabric. Subcut a **total of (18)** 2½" squares.

Note: You will have the following totals: (1) 4½" square, (1) 4" light red square, (2) 3½" x 8½" rectangles, (2) 3½" x 6½" rectangles, (16) 3" squares, (18) 2½" squares, and (16) 1½" squares.

From the green fabric, cut (1) 4" strip across the **width** of the fabric. Subcut a **total of (6)** 4" squares. Set the remaining fabric aside for the border.

From the black fabric scrap, cut a **total of (2)** 1½" squares.

From the background fabric, cut:
- (1) 4½" strip across the **width** of the fabric. Subcut (4) 4½" squares. Trim the remainder of the strip to 2½" and subcut (4) 2½" squares.

- (1) 4" strip across the **width** of the fabric. Subcut (7) 4" squares and (1) 4" x 2" rectangle. Cut the rectangle in half to create (2) 2" squares.

- (2) 3½" strips across the **width** of the fabric.
  ◦ Subcut 1 strip into (12) 3½" squares.

1 Arrange the 4 chevrons, the star center, and (4) 4½" background squares in 3 rows of 3 as shown.

2 Sew the units together in rows and press away from the chevrons. Nest the seams and sew the rows together. Press.

3 Arrange the 1 cardinal corner quadrant, the left tail unit, and the left cardinal half as shown.

4 Sew the 2 quadrants together and press. Then, sew the halves together. Press to complete the left cardinal block. Repeat to make the right cardinal block.

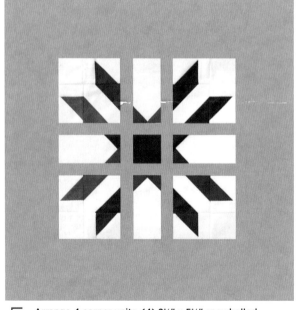

5 Arrange 4 corner units, (4) 2½" x 5½" snowballed rectangles, and (1) 2½" red square in 3 rows of 3 as shown.

6 Sew the units together in rows and press towards the squares. Nest the seams, sew the rows together, and press. Make 2.

3A

3B

3C

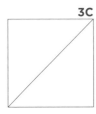

◦ Subcut 1 strip into (3) 3½" x 6½" rectangles, (2) 3½" x 5½" rectangles, and (3) 3½" x 3" rectangles. Trim the (3) 3½" x 3" rectangles to 3" square. Subcut (1) 3½" x 6½" rectangle into (2) 1½" x 6½" rectangles.

• (1) 3" strip across the **width** of the fabric. Subcut into (13) 3" squares.

• (2) 2½" strips across the **width** of the fabric. Subcut (4) 2½" x 5½" rectangles, (2) 2½" squares, and (10) 2½" x 1½" rectangles from each strip. Trim (4) 2½" x 1½" rectangles to 1½" square.

Note: You will have the following totals: (4) 4½" squares, (7) 4" squares, (2) 3½" x 6½" rectangles, (2) 3½" x 5½" rectangles, (12) 3½" squares, (16) 3" squares, (8) 2½" x 5½" rectangles, (8) 2½" squares, (16) 2½" x 1½" rectangles, (2) 1½" x 6½" rectangles, (2) 2" squares, and (4) 1½" squares.

2 make the half-square triangles

Mark a diagonal line from corner to corner on the reverse side of (7) 4" and (16) 3" background squares. **2A**

Lay a 4" marked square, right sides together, atop the 4" light red square. Sew on both sides of the marked line

using a ¼" seam allowance. Cut on the line. Use the trimmer to square each unit to 3½", then open and press—or press, then square to 3½" if you're not using the trimmer. These are the wing half-square triangles. **2B**

Repeat with the remaining 4" marked squares and (6) 4" green squares to **make 12** green half-square triangles. **2C**

Repeat with the (16) 3" marked squares and (16) 3" red squares to **make 32** small red half-square triangles. Square each to 2½". **2D**

3 snowball corners

Note: Some of the units made in this section are mirrors of 1 another. You may find it helpful to keep the mirrored units together for easier block construction later on. Pick up the (4) 1½" background squares and the 4½" red square. Fold each background square on the diagonal and finger press a crease. **3A**

Place a creased square on each corner of the 4½" red square, right sides facing. Sew on the creased lines, then trim the excess fabric ¼" away from each seam. Press towards the corners to make the star center. **3B**

97

Pick up (4) 3½" background squares, (2) 2" background squares, (2) 1½" black squares, (2) 3½" x 8½" red rectangles, (2) 3½" x 6½" red rectangles, and (2) 3½" x 5½" background rectangles. Fold each square in half on the diagonal and finger press a crease. **3C**

Lay a 3½" creased square and a 2" creased square on a 3½" x 8½" red rectangle, right sides facing, as shown. Snowball the corners as before to make the left body unit. **3D**

In the same manner, use another 3½" and the 2" creased background squares to snowball the opposite corners of the remaining 3½" x 8½" red rectangle as shown. This is the right body unit. **3E**

Snowball the ends of (2) 3½" x 6½" red rectangles using the 2 remaining creased 3½" squares as shown. The left tail unit has the snowballed corner on the left and the right tail unit has the snowballed corner on the right. **3F 3G**

Snowball the opposite upper corners of (2) 3½" x 5½" background rectangles as shown. The left beak unit has the corner added to the left side and the right beak unit has the corner added to the right side. **3H 3I**

Pick up 16 of the 2½" red squares, (16) 1½" red squares, (8) 2½" x 5½" background rectangles, and (8) 3½" background squares.

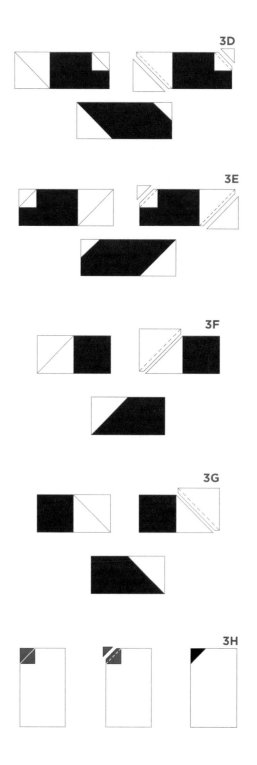

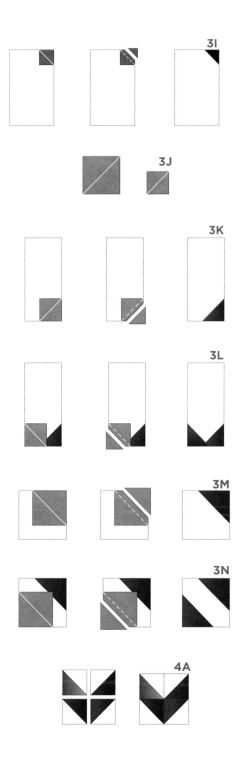

Fold each red square in half on the diagonal and finger press a crease. **3J**

Lay a 1½" red square atop a corner of a 2½" x 5½" background rectangle, right sides facing, as shown. Snowball the corner as before. **3K**

Repeat to snowball the adjacent corner, as shown, using a second 1½" red square. **Make 8** for the snowflakes. **3L**

Lay a 2½" red square atop a corner of a 3½" background square, right sides facing, as shown. Snowball the corner, similar to before. **3M**

Repeat to snowball the opposite corner, as shown, using a second 2½" red square. **Make 8** for the snowflakes. **3N**

4 sew star block

Select 16 small red half-square triangles. Arrange 4 units in a chevron as shown. Sew the units together in rows and press in opposite directions. Nest the seams and sew the rows together. Press. **Make 4** chevrons. **4A**

Arrange the 4 chevrons, the star center, and (4) 4½" background squares in 3 rows of 3 as shown. Sew the units together in rows and press away from the chevrons. Nest the seams and sew the rows together. Press. **4B 4C**

Star Block Size: 12½" unfinished, 12" finished

5 sew cardinal blocks

Pick up the 12 green half-square triangles, 2 wing half-square triangles, (2) 1½" x 6½" background rectangles, 2 tail units, 2 body units, 2 beak units, and (2) 3½" x 6½" background rectangles. Separate the units into those for the left block and those for the right.

Arrange 3 green half-square triangles and 1 wing half-square triangle as shown. Sew the units together in rows and press in opposite directions. Nest the seams and sew the rows together. Press. **Make 2** cardinal corner units and set them aside for now. **5A**

Sew the left body unit and 1 green half-square triangle together, as shown. Press towards the bottom. **5B**

Sew the left beak unit and 2 green half-square triangles together as shown. Press towards the top. **5C**

Sew the 2 units just made together as shown. Press. Sew (1) 1½" x 6½" background rectangle to the top of the unit. Press and set aside for now. **5D**

Sew the right body unit and 1 green half-square triangle together, as shown. Press towards the bottom. **5E**

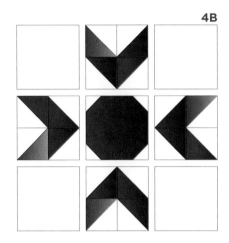

4B

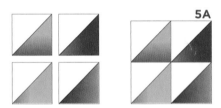

5A

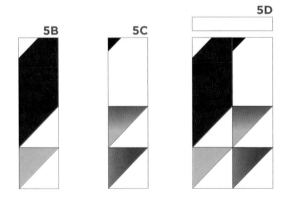

5B   5C   5D

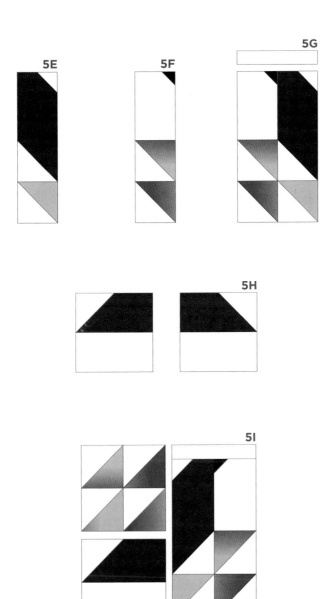

5E

5F

5G

5H

5I

Sew the right beak unit and 2 green half-square triangles together as shown. Press towards the top. **5F**

Sew the 2 units just made together as shown. Press. Sew (1) 1½" x 6½" background rectangle to the top of the unit. Press and set aside for now. **5G**

Sew (1) 3½" x 6½" background rectangle to the bottom of each tail unit and press. **5H**

Arrange the 1 cardinal corner quadrant, the left tail unit, and the left cardinal half as shown. Sew the 2 quadrants together and press. Then, sew the halves together. Press to complete the left cardinal block. **5I 5J**

In a similar fashion, sew the right cardinal block together. **5K**

Cardinal Block Size:
12½" unfinished, 12" finished

6 sew snowflake blocks

Pick up the (8) 2½" background squares, (16) 2½" x 1½" background rectangles, 16 small red half-square triangles, (8) 3½" snowballed squares, (8) 2½" x 5½"snowballed rectangles, and (2) 2½" red squares. Sew a 2½" x 1½" rectangle to the left side of a small red half-square triangle as shown. **Make 8** A units. **6A**

Sew a 2½" x 1½" rectangle to the left side of a small red half-square triangle as shown. Notice the red portion of the half-square triangle is now in the upper left corner. **Make 8** B units. **6B**

Arrange (1) 2½" background square, an A unit, a B unit, and a 3½" snowballed square as shown. Sew the units together in rows and press in opposite directions. Nest the seams and sew the rows together. Press. **Make 8** corner units. **6C**

Arrange 4 corner units, (4) 2½" x 5½" snowballed rectangles, and (1) 2½" red square in 3 rows of 3 as shown. Sew the units together in rows and press towards the squares. Nest the seams, sew the rows together, and press. **Make 2**. **6D 6E**

Snowflake Block Size:
12½" unfinished, 12" finished

7 arrange & sew
Arrange the blocks into **1 row of 5 blocks** as shown in the diagram on the left. Notice that the cardinals face the center.

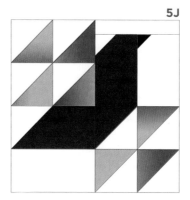

5J

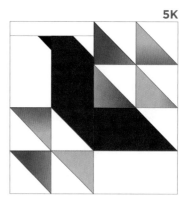

5K

6A

6B

6C

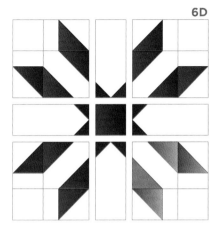

6D

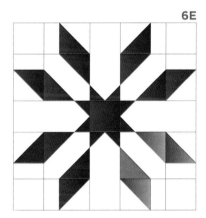

6E

Sew the blocks together to form the row and press.

8 border

Cut (4) 2½" strips across the width of the green ombré fabric. Sew 3 strips together to make 1 long strip. Trim the top and bottom borders from this long strip and the side borders from the single strip. Refer to Borders (pg. 118) in the Construction Basics to measure, cut, and attach the borders. The lengths are approximately 60½" for the top and bottom and 16½" for the sides. Notice the top and bottom borders are sewn on first and then the side borders.

9 quilt & bind

Layer the project with batting and backing, then quilt. After the quilting is complete, see Construction Basics (pg. 118) to finish your project.

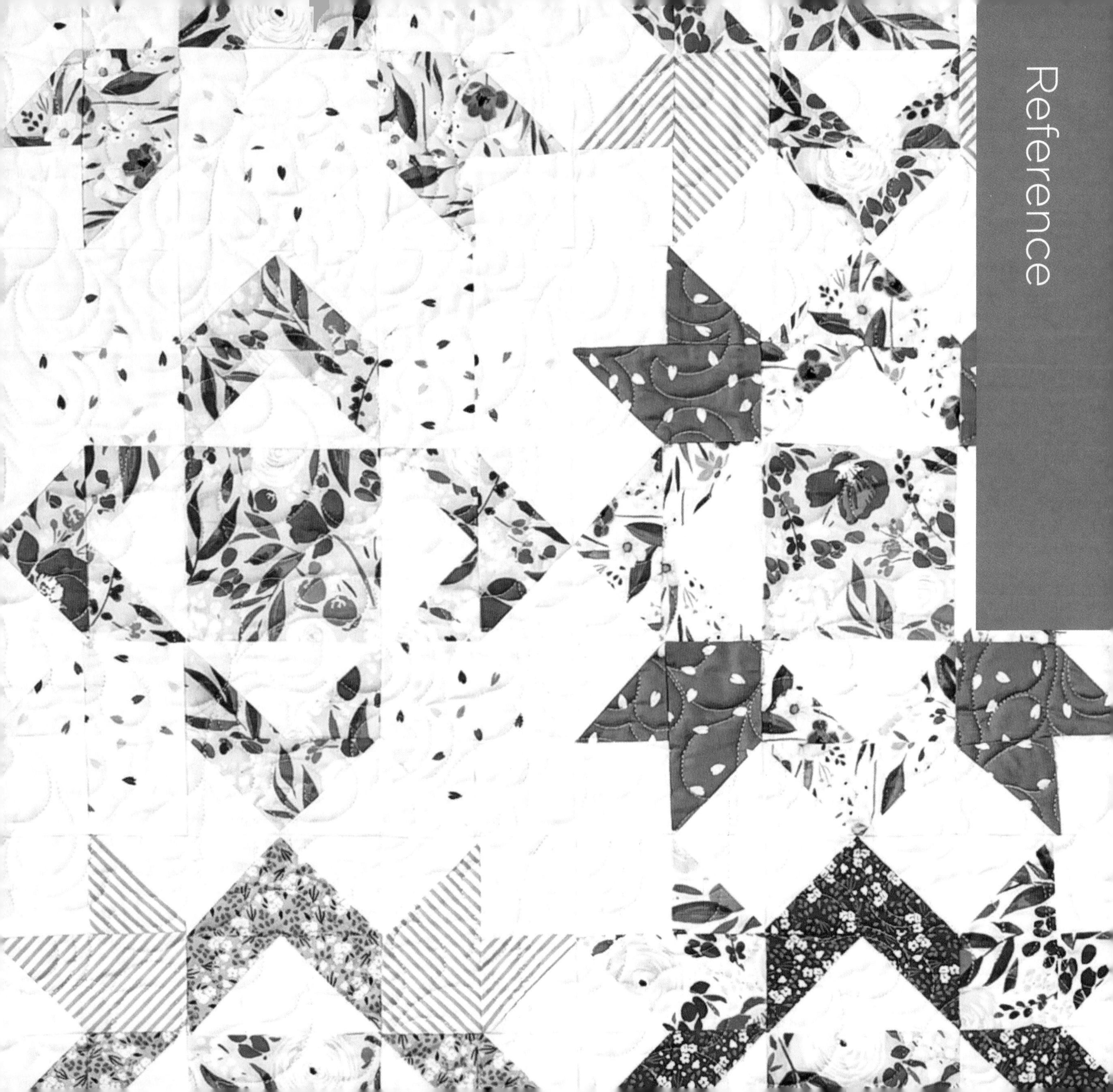

E'toile de France
designed by Susan Hudson

QUILT SIZE
92" x 92"

BLOCK SIZE
58½" unfinished, 58" finished

QUILT TOP
6 different fabrics are needed for the star & pieced borders
• Fabric A - ½ yard
• Fabric B - ¾ yard
• Fabric C - 1 yard
• Fabric D - 1 yard
• Fabric E - 1¼ yards
• Fabric F - 1 yard
4½ yards background fabric
   - includes borders

BINDING
¾ yard

BACKING
8½ yards - vertical seam(s)
   or 2¾ yards of 108" wide

SAMPLE QUILT
La Vie Boheme
   by French General for Moda Fabrics

PATTERN
P. 18

Happy Little Spools

QUILT SIZE
58" x 68"

BLOCK SIZE
4½" x 7" unfinished,
  4" x 6½" finished

QUILT TOP
1 package of 5" solid squares
¾ yard accent fabric
2½ yards background fabric*
  - includes sashing and inner border

BORDER
¾ yard

BINDING
¾ yard

BACKING
3¾ yards - horizontal seam(s)

__Note:__ 1 roll of 1½" background strips and ¾ yard background fabric can be substituted. You will need to cut (6) additional 1½" background strips and add them to your roll, then follow directions for the remaining (12) 1" strips.

SAMPLE QUILT
Kona Cotton - Bright Rainbow Palette
by Robert Kaufman

QUILTING PATTERN
A Notion to Sew

PATTERN
P. 26

Lady of the Lake

QUILT SIZE
70" x 70"

BLOCK SIZE
10½" unfinished, 10" finished

QUILT TOP
1 package of 10" print squares
1 package of 10" background squares

BORDER
1¼ yards

BINDING
¾ yard

BACKING
4½ yards - vertical seam(s)
   or 2¼ yards of 108" wide

OTHER
Clearly Perfect Slotted
   Trimmers A and B or
   Bloc Loc 6½" Square Up Ruler

SAMPLE QUILT
Gratitude and Grace by Kim Diehl
   for Henry Glass

QUILTING PATTERN
Bo Dangle

PATTERN
P. 32

Mother's Choice Remake

QUILT SIZE
63" x 75"

BLOCK SIZE
12½" unfinished, 12" finished

QUILT TOP
1 roll of 2½" print strips
1 roll of 2½" background strips

INNER BORDER
½ yard

OUTER BORDER
1¾ yards - includes block
    center squares

BINDING
¾ yard

BACKING
4¾ yards - vertical seam(s)
    or 2½ yards of 108" wide

SAMPLE QUILT
Cora by Tessie Fay
    for Windham Fabrics

QUILTING PATTERN
Deb's Feathers

PATTERN
P. 38

Sassy Spools

QUILT SIZE
72½" x 81½"

BLOCK SIZE
10½" unfinished, 10" finished

QUILT TOP
1 package of 10" print squares
½ yard white solid fabric
1½ yards accent fabric
 - includes inner border

OUTER BORDER
1½ yards

BINDING
¾ yard

BACKING
5 yards - vertical seam(s)
 or 2½ yards of 108" wide

SAMPLE QUILT
Stitch by Lori Holt of Bee in my
 Bonnet for Riley Blake Designs

QUILTING PATTERN
Spools of Thread

PATTERN
P. 44

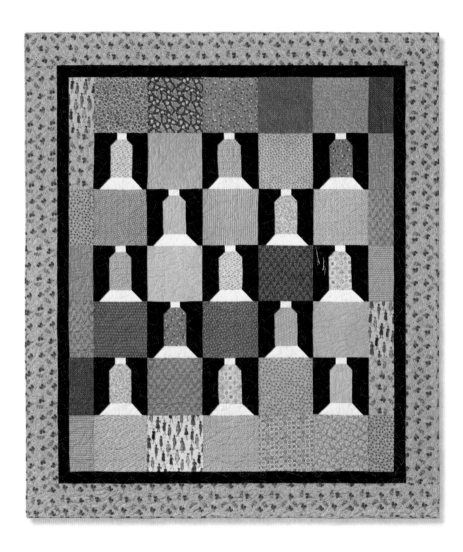

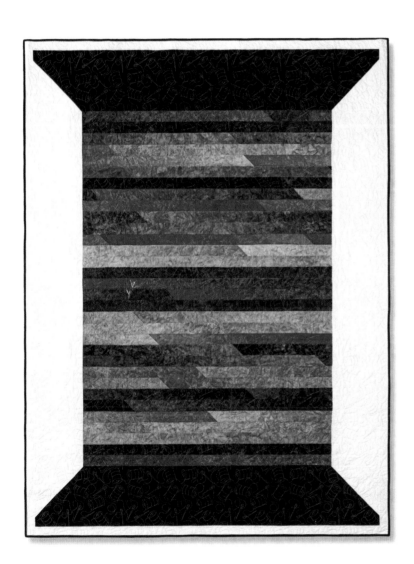

World's Largest Spool of Thread

QUILT SIZE
72½" x 91"

QUILT TOP
1 roll 2½" print strips
1½ yards accent fabric
2 yards background fabric
  - includes border

BINDING
¾ yard

BACKING
5½ yards - vertical seam(s)
  or 2¾ yards of 108" wide

SAMPLE QUILT
Artisan Batiks - Patina Handpaints
  by Lunn Studios for Robert Kaufman

QUILTING PATTERN
Spools of Thread

PATTERN
P. 50

Talavera Tile

Studio Star + Fancy Flight
(Blocks Only)

STUDIO STAR BLOCK SIZE
9½" unfinished, 9" finished

FANCY FLIGHT BLOCK SIZE
2½" x 4½" unfinished,
2" x 4" finished

BLOCK SUPPLIES - STUDIO STAR
(1) 10" fabric B square
(2) 10" fabric C squares
(1) 10" fabric D square
(1) 2½" fabric F strips
   (cut from yardage)
(4) 2½" fabric G strips
   (cut from yardage)

BLOCK SUPPLIES - FANCY FLIGHT
(1) 10" fabric B square
(2) 10" fabric D squares
(1) 10" fabric E square
(4) 2½" fabric G strips
   (cut from yardage)

Note*: Fabric A is not used in Part 4.*

SAMPLE QUILT
Circle Burst Wilmington Essentials
   by Wilmington Prints
Vintage Texture Wilmington Essentials
   by Wilmington Prints

QUILTING PATTERN
Free Swirls

PATTERN
P. 54

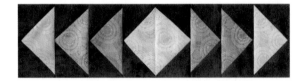

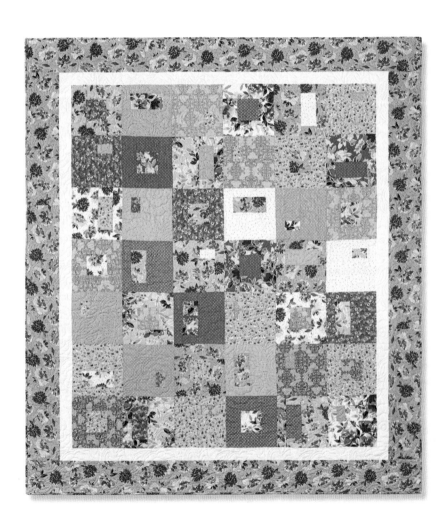

Skylight

QUILT SIZE
66" x 74½"

BLOCK SIZE
9" unfinished, 8½" finished

QUILT TOP
1 package of 10" print squares

INNER BORDER
½ yard

OUTER BORDER
1¼ yards

BINDING
¾ yard

BACKING
4¾ yards - vertical seam(s)
    or 2½ yards of 108" wide

SAMPLE QUILT
Lucy Jane by Lila Tuller
    for Riley Blake

QUILTING PATTERN
Just Roses

PATTERN
P. 72

Summer Squares

QUILT SIZE
67" x 67"

BLOCK SIZE
7" unfinished, 6½" finished

QUILT TOP
1 roll of 2½" print strips
½ yard of gray fabric
½ yard of white fabric

BORDER
1½ yards

BINDING
¾ yard

BACKING
4¼ yards – vertical seam(s)
    or 2¼ yards of 108" wide

OTHER
Clearly Perfect Slotted Trimmer B2
Spray starch - recommended

SAMPLE QUILT
Awakenings by Stephanie Ryan
    for Wilmington Prints
Kona Cotton - White
    for Robert Kaufman
Bella Solids - Graphite
    for Moda Fabrics

QUILTING PATTERN
Curly Twirly Flowers

PATTERN
P. 78

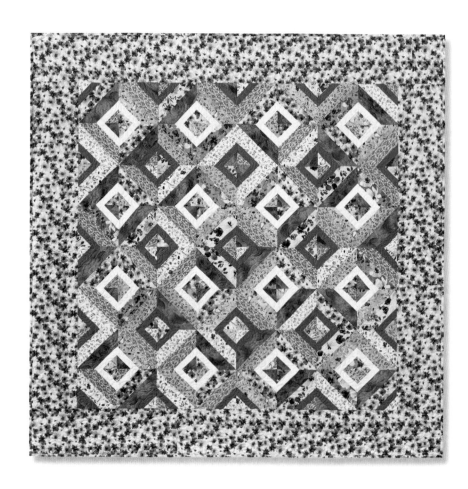

60 Degree Stars

QUILT SIZE
75" x 85"

BLOCK SIZE
8⅜" x 19⅛" unfinished half-hexagon,
7⅞" x 18¼" finished half-hexagon

QUILT TOP
1 roll of 2½" print strips
4¾ yards of background fabric
  - includes inner border

OUTER BORDER
1½ yards

BINDING
¾ yard

BACKING
5¼ yards – vertical seam(s)
  or 2¾ yards of 108" wide

OTHER
Missouri Star 8" Equilateral
  60 Degree Triangle Ruler
Spray starch - recommended

SAMPLE QUILT
Wilmington Essentials - Bubble Up
  by Wilmington Prints

QUILTING PATTERN
Paisley Feathers

PATTERN
P. 88

Cardinal Table Runner

PROJECT SIZE
64" x 16"

BLOCK SIZES
12½" unfinished, 12" finished

PROJECT TOP
1 yard red ombré fabric
½ yard green ombré fabric
  - includes border
2" x 4" rectangle black fabric scrap
¾ yard background fabric

BINDING
½ yard

BACKING
1½ yards - vertical seam(s)

OTHER
Clearly Perfect Slotted Trimmer - A

SAMPLE PROJECT
Gelato - Ombre Red and Ombre Green by Maywood Studio

Grunge Basics - White Paper by BasicGrey for Moda Fabrics

QUILTING PATTERN
Christmas Paisley

PATTERN
P. 94

Construction Basics

General Quilting

- All seams are ¼" inch unless directions specify differently.
- Cutting instructions are given at the point when cutting is required.
- Precuts are not prewashed, therefore do not prewash other fabrics in the project.
- All strips are cut width of fabric.
- Remove all selvages.

Press Seams

- Use a steam iron on the cotton setting.
- Press the seam just as it was sewn right sides together. This "sets" the seam.
- With dark fabric on top, lift the dark fabric and press back.
- The seam allowance is pressed toward the dark side. Some patterns may direct otherwise for certain situations.
- Follow pressing arrows in the diagrams when indicated.
- Press toward borders. Pieced borders may need otherwise.
- Press diagonal seams open on binding to reduce bulk.

Borders

- Always measure the quilt top 3x before cutting borders.
- Start measuring about 4" in from each side and through the center vertically.
- Take the average of those 3 measurements.
- Cut 2 border strips to that size. Piece strips together if needed.
- Attach 1 to either side of the quilt.

- Position the border fabric on top as you sew. The feed dogs can act like rufflers. Having the border on top will prevent waviness and keep the quilt straight.
- Repeat this process for the top and bottom borders, measuring the width 3 times.
- Include the newly attached side borders in your measurements.
- Press toward the borders.

Binding

find a video tutorial at: www.msqc.co/006

- Use 2½" strips for binding.
- Sew strips end-to-end into 1 long strip with diagonal seams, aka the plus sign method (next). Press the seams open.
- Fold in half lengthwise, wrong sides together, and press.
- The entire length should equal the outside dimension of the quilt plus 15" - 20."

Plus Sign Method

find a video tutorial at: www.msqc.co/001

- Lay 1 strip across the other as if to make a plus sign, right sides together.
- Sew from top inside to bottom outside corners crossing the intersections of fabric as you sew.
- Trim excess to ¼" seam allowance.
- Press seam open.

Attach Binding

- Match raw edges of folded binding to the quilt top edge.
- Leave a 10" tail at the beginning.
- Use a ¼" seam allowance.
- Start in the middle of a long straight side.

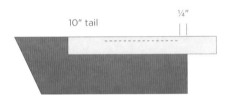

Miter Corners

- Stop sewing ¼" before the corner.
- Move the quilt out from under the presser foot.
- Clip the threads.
- Flip the binding up at a 90° angle to the edge just sewn.
- Fold the binding down along the next side to be sewn, aligning raw edges.
- The fold will lie along the edge just completed.
- Begin sewing on the fold.

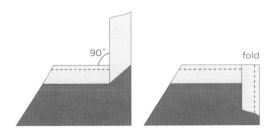

Close Binding

MSQC recommends The Binding Tool from TQM Products to finish binding perfectly every time.

- Stop sewing when you have 12" left to reach the start.
- Where the binding tails come together, trim the excess leaving only 2½" of overlap.
- It helps to pin or clip the quilt together at the 2 points where the binding starts and stops. This takes the pressure off of the binding tails while you work.
- Use the plus sign method to sew the 2 binding ends together, except this time when making the plus sign, match the edges. Using a pencil, mark your sewing line because you won't be able to see where the corners intersect. Sew across.

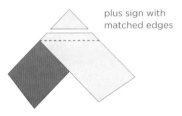

plus sign with matched edges

- Trim off the excess; press the seam open.
- Fold in half wrong sides together, and align all raw edges to the quilt top.
- Sew this last binding section to the quilt. Press.
- Turn the folded edge of the binding around to the back of the quilt and tack into place with an invisible stitch or machine stitch if you wish.